THE POLITICS
AND LAW OF
TERM
LIMITS

THE POLITICS AND LAW OF TERM LIMITS

edited by
Edward H. Crane and Roger Pilon

CATO
INSTITUTE
Washington, D.C.

Library of Congress Cataloging-in-Publication Data

The politics and law of term limits : edited by Edward H. Crane and
  Roger Pilon.
    p.   cm.
    Includes bibliographical references.
    ISBN 1-882577-12-4 (cloth) : $19.95. — ISBN 1-882577-13-2 (paper) :
$10.95
    1. United States. Congress—Term of office.   I. Crane, Edward H.,
1944–   . II. Pilon, Roger.
JK1140.P65   1994
328.73′.073—dc20   94-35217
                                                    CIP

Cover Design by Colin Moore.

Printed in the United States of America.

CATO INSTITUTE
1000 Massachusetts Ave., N.W.
Washington, D.C. 20001

Contents

PART I INTRODUCTION

1. An American Debate
   Edward H. Crane and Roger Pilon   3

2. Term Limits
   George F. Will   15

PART II THE POLITICS OF TERM LIMITS

3. From the Voters with Care
   Paul Jacob   27

4. Term Limits: Not the Answer to What Ails
   Politics
   Becky Cain   45

5. Restoring "The University in Rotation": An
   Essay in Defense of Term Limitation
   Mark P. Petracca   57

6. Congressional Term Limits: A Bad Idea Whose
   Time Should Never Come
   Thomas E. Mann   83

PART III THE LAW OF TERM LIMITS

7. The Constitutionality of State-Imposed Term
   Limits for Federal Office
   Lloyd N. Cutler   99

8. State Term-Limits Laws and the Constitution
   John G. Kester   109

9. Congressional Term Limits and the
   Constitution
   Daniel Hays Lowenstein   125

10. A Commentary on the Constitutionality of
    Term Limits
    Ronald D. Rotunda   141

INDEX   157

CONTRIBUTORS   163

Part I

Introduction

1. An American Debate

Edward H. Crane and Roger Pilon

It is no overstatement to say that the term-limits movement—a national, grassroots effort to limit the terms of elected officials at all levels of government—is emerging as one of the most important political developments in this nation in a very long time. Reaching beyond such political staples as crime, economic policy, or welfare reform, term limitation speaks in fundamental ways to the question of how we will govern ourselves. Although the political establishment has often been slow, for understandable reasons, to acknowledge the movement, it can be ignored no longer.

Coming out of Middle America in September of 1990, when the voters of Oklahoma decided to limit the terms of their state legislators, term limits moved west in November of that year when California did the same while Colorado limited the terms of both its state and its federal legislators. Two years later, measures to limit the terms of federal legislators passed, often by overwhelming margins, in all 14 states in which they were on the ballot. With 7, and possibly 10, more states expected to follow suit this fall, voters in 16 states have now limited the terms of their state legislators, while hundreds of counties and cities, including New York and Los Angeles, the nation's largest cities, have limited the terms of their elected officials as well. As we go to press, a term-limits measure has just been certified for the ballot for this fall in Washington, D.C., which means that the term-limits movement has come at last even to the nation's capital.

But the movement has not been without opposition. Losing time after time at the polls, the political establishment that would be affected most directly by term limitation has sought relief in the courts, trying repeatedly to keep term-limits measures from the ballot, then to have those measures declared unconstitutional after the voters have spoken. Perhaps the most celebrated such effort, dubbed "Foley v. Voters," was a suit brought by Speaker of the

3

House Thomas S. Foley, a 30-year incumbent of the U.S. House of Representatives, to have the term-limits measure that Washington state voters passed in 1992 declared unconstitutional. That suit is now before the U.S. Court of Appeals for the Ninth Circuit.

In the meantime, the Foley case has been overtaken by another, a suit brought by a number of interested parties in President Clinton's home state of Arkansas to overturn the term-limits measure that 60 percent of the voters of that state had passed in 1992. When the Arkansas Supreme Court, in a split decision, struck down the provisions of that measure that limited the terms of the state's congressional delegation, U.S. Term Limits, one of the defendants in the suit and the leading national organization promoting term limits, immediately appealed the decision to the United States Supreme Court. On June 20, 1994, the Court agreed to hear the case. Oral argument is scheduled for this fall.

To address both the political and the legal questions that the term-limits movement has raised, the Cato Institute's Center for Constitutional Studies held a conference on December 1, 1993, on "The Politics and Law of Term Limits." Drawing together some of the nation's leading experts on the subject, the conference featured both proponents and opponents of term limits and included heads of activist organizations, public policy analysts, and legal practitioners and scholars. The conference was aired nationally on the C-SPAN television network, and the spirited debate that ensued reflected, in our view, a prime example of the value of civil policy discourse. The essays that follow are based on the papers presented at the conference and are offered here in the spirit of continuing that debate.

The volume begins with an essay by the noted syndicated columnist and television commentator George F. Will, who may well be the nation's most visible proponent of congressional term limitation. A student of the American revolutionary period who originally was an opponent of term limitation, Will is a self-described American Tory who once wrote, "A great state can not be run by 'citizen legislators' and amateur administrators."

In recent years, however, George Will the Tory has become rather more George Will the Jeffersonian. The enthusiasm Will once had for the strong central government of the Hamiltonian vision— explaining his earlier opposition to congressional term limitation—

4

is today directed toward a more populist vision that emphasizes the need for citizen legislatures if we are to have a truly representative democracy.

Although Will thinks the Founding Fathers were right to not include them in the Constitution, he writes of term limits that "what justifies them now is the nature of the modern state." With the advent of the "interventionist state" in the post–Civil War era, Will sees legislative service as increasingly attractive to those who would like to make a career in government, creating in turn a political class peopled by professional politicians who by definition represent something other than civil society.

Unlike many conservative supporters of term limitation who believe that the institution of limits will lead to a reduction of government meddling in society, Will reserves judgment on the point— suggesting even that the opposite might well prove true. He does believe, however, that respect for Congress itself will grow if the institution is seen by the public to be more a citizen legislature than a political ruling class.

As for measures to limit campaign giving and spending or to have the government finance campaigns—which opponents of term limits often propose as alternatives to term limits—Will finds those alternatives "facially unconstitutional." Moreover, such measures inevitably help incumbents, who already have such advantages as incumbency, name recognition, franking privileges, and free television studios.

Although Will reminds those who believe term limitation to be anti-democratic that America has "never flirted for a minute with untrameled majoritarianism," many term-limit proponents, while granting Will's point, nevertheless believe that term limits will enhance the democratic process. Most contested races, they point out, are for open seats, and the number of open seats will be dramatically increased through the term-limitation process, leading to greater voter interest and involvement in elections. George Will's opening contribution to this book is a persuasive case for term limitation from someone who is less interested in bashing Congress than in restoring respect to an institution that is fundamental to the limited, albeit important, sphere of human affairs subject to democratic rule.

Two of the leading grassroots organizations engaged in the congressional term-limitation battle are represented in this volume by

Paul Jacob, executive director of U.S. Term Limits, and Becky Cain, president of the League of Women Voters. As already noted, U.S. Term Limits is the principal national organization behind the term-limits movement and an appellant in the Supreme Court case that will decide whether states may limit the terms of their congressional delegations. The League of Women Voters has steadfastly opposed term limits and will file an amicus brief in the Supreme Court supporting those who want to strike down the Arkansas term-limits initiative, despite numerous polls indicating that support for term limits among women is even higher than among men.

(As we go to press, the National Women's Political Caucus has just released a study, reaching back to 1972, that shows that "success rates for male and female candidates were virtually identical at every level of office" and that incumbency, not sex, determines electoral success. Noting that House incumbents won 16 times as often as challengers, the study's author, NWPC executive director Jody Newman, added that "winning has nothing to do with sex and everything to do with incumbency. In order to win, women have had to defeat a sitting [usually male] incumbent, or wait for him to retire, resign, or die.")

In his essay, Paul Jacob makes a powerful case for term limits, then aggressively addresses the issues raised by term-limit opponents. To those who criticize the supposedly anti-democratic aspects of term limitation, Jacob points to polls that demonstrate between 75 and 80 percent support for them. In fact, pollsters are struck by the relatively little demographic variation they find within the overwhelming support for term limitation. Women support limits slightly more than men, blacks somewhat more than whites, and conservatives just a bit more than liberals. But in virtually all groups, support for term limits exceeds 70 percent.

The exception, not surprisingly, is provided by the political establishment. Jacob cites a Gallup poll among congressional staff, Washington corporate lobbyists, and federal bureaucrats that showed all three groups opposed to term limitation. But that opposition affords only another rejoinder to critics of term limits: to those who argue that under a term-limited Congress the power of such groups would be enhanced, Jacob responds that if that were the case, why are those groups opposed to term limits?

To the claim that term limitation reflects simply a visceral reaction to high levels of congressional corruption, Jacob points to existing limits on the terms of the president and 37 state governors. Apart from their concern to apply limits to Congress as well, however, voters doubtless are frustrated by congressional scandal, including the unwillingness of Congress even to address the question of term limitation. In fact, Congress's overt antagonism toward term limitation, and its practice of exempting itself from the laws it imposes on the rest of us, only underscores the need to bring some humility to the institution. In Jacob's view that means rotation in office and a citizen legislature.

To Becky Cain, "Term limits are a smoke screen, a simplistic answer to hard questions about our government . . . ." She provides an articulate litany of arguments that term-limit opponents typically put forth: we already have term limits, they're called elections; term limits are a "meat ax" approach to public policy; term limits will deprive us of our most experienced legislators; and term limits will turn power over to congressional staff and insiders. Cain devotes a good portion of her argument, however, to the need for such reforms as public financing of campaigns and public school requirements that get students involved in political activism in order to pass social studies courses. The views of the League of Women Voters on such issues parallel those of another major activist organization, Common Cause.

From the policy analysts, the essays by Mark Petracca, professor of political science at the University of California at Irvine, and Thomas Mann, senior fellow at the Brookings Institution, offer forceful, intelligent cases for their respective positions, for and against term limitation. Interestingly, both focus on two primary issues: the historical record concerning the term-limitation debate and the question of whether "professionalism" in politics is good or bad.

Petracca traces support for the concept of rotation in office from Aristotle and Cicero through the Articles of Confederation. He argues that the historical case for rotation in office rests on the desirability of "returning officeholders to private station," the increased opportunity for more citizens to participate in the political arena, and the enhanced quality of representation that results from a system in which officeholders are truly "representative."

Petracca then raises the more problematic question of why the Framers neglected to include term limits in the Constitution, suggesting that they viewed the issue as too specific for what was obviously a very general document and that, in any case, it was assumed that rotation in office would be the norm—as indeed it was until this century. In fact, the "professional legislator" is a wholly modern phenomenon. It was not until 1901, Petracca notes, that the average number of terms served by House members rose above two. More than half of the House membership during the entire second half of the 19th century was composed of first-term congressmen. Today, about a third of the House is composed of members who have served for 14 years or more, a pattern one finds in the Senate as well.

This trend toward "professionalism" in politics should disturb anyone concerned about the future of representative democracy. Sociologists have noted that professionalism in any field tends toward undesirable side effects—professional jargon, distance, unintelligibility to laymen. Perhaps such distancing can be justified in some fields, but politics is surely not one of them—assuming representative democracy is a desirable objective. In a democracy, Petracca argues, "professional representation" is an oxymoron. Echoing George Will's theme, Petracca concludes that term limitation should be enacted "on the basis of principles necessary to enhance the democratic character of the American republic."

To the Brookings Institution's Thomas Mann, nothing could be further from the truth. Claiming that "the crux of the case for term limits is a rejection of professionalism in politics," Mann sets out to defend such professionalism—or what he calls "legislative careerism." As the world becomes more complex, the need for specialization grows, he argues, from which professionalism follows. Moreover, only professional politicians are likely to be "committed to the larger purposes of the institution of which they are a part." In Mann's view, the professional legislator is more likely to act in a manner consistent with deliberative democracy.

Defending a primary target of the term-limits movement, seniority, Mann argues that the elimination of seniority as the basis for selecting congressional leadership would "devalue the authority of those positions." Here, perhaps, we have basic agreement among the various participants in this debate concerning a likely outcome of term limitation—and a rather basic disagreement concerning the value of that outcome. Mann also takes issue with certain points made by Paul Jacob, asserting that term limitation will not increase the competitiveness of congressional races and that there is no correlation between pork-barrel spending and congressional careerism.

Whatever the merits of term limits, there can be no question, as indicated earlier, about where the overwhelming majority of the American people stand on the issue. As George Will once noted, "To the question 'Where most recently have term limits passed?' the answer is: 'Wherever most recently people were permitted to vote on them.' " The operative word here, of course, is "permitted." For again, when not ignoring the term-limits movement, the political establishment has often turned to the courts to try to strike term-limits measures from the ballot—or to have them found unconstitutional once they have passed. We turn, then, from the political to the legal side of the issue and to the specific question of whether, under the U.S. Constitution, the voters of a state may limit the terms of their congressional delegation.

To address that question, our conference heard from two distinguished lawyers with long histories of Washington experience and two noted legal scholars, both of whom had written on the subject. Lloyd Cutler is "an old Washington hand" who served as legal counsel to President Jimmy Carter and now is acting counsel to President Clinton. His counterpart, John Kester, served in the Department of Defense in both the Nixon and Carter administrations and now is lead counsel for U.S. Term Limits. He will be arguing the term-limits case this fall before the Supreme Court.

On the academic side, Daniel Lowenstein served in the administration of California Governor Jerry Brown before joining the faculty of the UCLA School of Law. Ronald Rotunda, coauthor of a standard casebook as well as a four-volume treatise on constitutional law, is the Albert E. Jenner, Jr., professor of law at the University of Illinois College of Law.

Although the term-limits movement has been growing now for more than four years, there is still a relative paucity of legal analysis of the subject. One often hears some legal commentator say, offhandedly, that of course term limits are unconstitutional, yet the analysis one finds usually tends in the other direction. Perhaps that indicates only that the legal establishment, like the political establishment, has been slow to respond, or it may indicate instead that the argument for unconstitutionality is rather weaker than at first thought. In any event, the question will likely be one of first impression for the Court, which is why an open mind on the matter is so crucial.

But an open mind is never entirely open, of course, or without some presumption, even in law. One would hope that in a free society, in ordinary legal affairs, the presumption would always be on the side of individual liberty. In political affairs, when it is a question of whether the individual, as voter, may order his affairs as he thinks best, here too the presumption would seem to be on the side of liberty. At the least, the question ought to be whether there is anything in the Constitution that would override that liberty.

The importance of presumptions, and of framing an issue, is brought out clearly in the essays by our legal practitioners. Lloyd Cutler, for example, assumes that term limits are "qualifications for federal office." He then looks to the constitutional debates to conclude—with the Supreme Court in *Powell v. McCormack*, as he reads the case—that "the Founders agreed upon a final list of qualifications, and determined that they should be exclusive." In particular, "a member-elect who meets the constitutional qualifications cannot be excluded." (Query: Are the rules for exclusion of members-elect the same as the rules for ballot access?) To support his conclusions further, Cutler draws upon both the political and the legal record that runs from post-revolutionary American state constitutions through the Constitutional Convention and the ratification debates to the post-ratification experience. Finding the record clear on the point, he adds finally that efforts by supporters of term limits to recast them not as qualifications (controlled by Article I, sections 2 and 3 of the Constitution) but as "ballot-access restrictions" (controlled by Article I, section 4, which gives states the power to regulate the time, place, and manner of elections) are "entirely without merit"; however denominated, Cutler concludes, a term-limits measure "clearly imposes a qualification."

By contrast, John Kester begins not with the early constitutional debates, as interpreted by the Court in *Powell*, but with the text and structure of the Constitution. Finding the text "silent on the subject" of term limits, he frames the issue by noting that "the Constitution structurally limits state lawmaking far less than it limits the U.S. Congress." Thus, the question is whether anything in the Constitution prohibits the voters of a state from limiting the terms of the members of their congressional delegation. Taking sharp exception to Cutler, Kester argues that "a 'ballot-access' law does not amount to a qualification for holding office," nor are sections 2 and 3 of Article I of the Constitution properly called "the Qualifications

Clauses," for they set forth *dis*qualifications. And those disqualifications can hardly be thought to be exclusive, both because of the logic of the language and because elsewhere in the Constitution we find other disqualifications for office. Unsupported by either text or history, the idea of exclusivity seems to have sprung, without authority, from Joseph Story, Kester notes, after which it was repeated by lower courts, but never addressed directly by the Supreme Court. What authority is drawn from *Powell*, he adds, arises from a misreading of the opinion, for the case "had nothing to do with state regulation of elections," or even with congressional regulation, but with the power of a single chamber of Congress, when sitting as "judge," to pass on the qualifications of one of its members. Finally, Fourteenth Amendment objections to term limits are weaker still, Kester concludes; indeed, were they to prevail, a huge number of state election regulations, many already approved by the Court, would have to go.

Turning now to the academic contributors, here too we see the importance of presumptions. Thus, Daniel Lowenstein begins by asserting that congressional term limits "violate the qualifications clauses of the Constitution," an assertion he defends by claiming that proponents, to show constitutionality, must establish at least one of three propositions: (1) that states are permitted to establish additional qualifications; (2) that term limits are not qualifications but regulations of election procedures or candidacy; or (3) that ballot-access restrictions do not evade the qualifications clause or violate the First and Fourteenth Amendments. Like Cutler, Lowenstein draws heavily upon *Powell v. McCormack*, concluding that proponents can establish none of those propositions, from which it follows that congressional term limits are unconstitutional. But does that follow? Or is it rather for term-limits *opponents* to show unconstitutionality? Lowenstein adduces a wide range of arguments toward that end. But in the end the distribution of the burden of proof—and the implications respecting constitutional structure—may be as important, and decisive, as the substantive arguments.

Ronald Rotunda frames the issue quite simply: Does anything in the Constitution or in Supreme Court case law preclude term limitation? With respect to the Constitution, he focuses on the qualifications clause, concluding from text and history "that the most natural reading . . . is that it sets forth necessary, but not exclusive, qualifications." That echo of Kester is repeated on the case-law side of the question, where Rotunda concludes that term-limits opponents have misread *Powell*: when exercising its power to exclude, pursuant to its power to judge the election returns of its members, Congress may not add qualifications "in the guise of ad hoc discipline of its members." This reading is a far cry from the broad reading many have given the case.

Of particular interest in Rotunda's essay, however, is the passage he cites from Jefferson, which Story had cited as a view that opposed his own on the qualifications clause:

> Jefferson argued that if it is the rule of interpretation that, when the Constitution "assumes a single power out of many," we "should consider it as assuming the whole," then the Constitution "would vest the general government with a mass of powers never contemplated."

We return thus to the question of presumptions and the structure of the Constitution. As with so much in law, the framing of the term-limits question may prove crucial to its legal outcome.

In recent years the Cato Institute has held seminars and produced studies on congressional term limitation that have convinced the editors of this volume of the wisdom of what the Founders called "rotation in office." We will conclude this introduction, therefore, with two arguments in support of congressional term limits that are only obliquely addressed in this volume.

The first concerns the "adverse selection" that occurs under current political arrangements. In considering today whether to run for Congress, ordinary citizens who might constitute a truly representative legislature face a discouraging prospect. On one hand, under the current system there are very few open seats and ousting an incumbent is next to impossible. On the other hand, a considerable commitment of time is required before one has any influence in a Congress run under today's seniority system. Out of a sense of civic duty someone might be willing to commit two, four, or even six years to serving in the House of Representatives, but not if others are going to be setting the agenda. Committee chairmanships are awarded today to those who have been in the House for an average of 19 years.

Ironically, the kind of person we should have in Congress is the person who would prefer to be in the productive, private sector.

That kind of person is likely to be a good representative of private, civil society, as opposed to political society. But the prospect of spending a dozen years or more as a politician is what keeps such people from running for office. By contrast, the kind of person who eagerly anticipates spending the rest of his life in politics is not likely to be "representative" of his community.

With real congressional term limits—three terms in the House, two terms in the Senate—there would be a more open, collegial culture in Congress, a culture that would be inviting to those who would be more representative of their community than is now the case. We suspect, in fact, that under a limit of three terms in the House, many people would serve for only one term, as was common during our nation's first century.

Beyond the adverse selection issue, however, lies another that urges term limitation. We are all familiar with the phenomenon of legislative logrolling, whereby one legislator agrees to vote for another legislator's bill in return for support for his own bill. That process occurs on a regular basis in Congress and is a leading generator of pork-barrel legislation. Indeed, Tony Coelho, new senior advisor to the Democratic National Committee, has just been quoted in *Roll Call*, "the Newspaper of Capitol Hill," as saying that "the most important thing for the Members to do today is concentrate on adopting legislation and being able to go home and run on something."

But there is more to logrolling than the endless generation of legislation. Typically, congressmen agree to support each other's bills and agree further not to try to have repealed any law that others have sponsored. Indeed, there is an ethic in the current congressional culture that sharply rebukes those who deign to alter or repeal legislation of another congressman. The true gridlock in Congress is thus not related to the members' inability to pass laws. Rather, gridlock manifests itself in the inability of Congress to repeal the huge inventory of previously passed laws that are doing actual damage to our society.

With the passage of term limitation, the culture in Congress is likely to change radically. One positive element of that change will be a greatly enhanced willingness and ability in Congress to address that body's past mistakes, both liberal and conservative, and clean up the deadwood that is such a burden on both economic growth and personal liberty. Absent term limitation, however, the culture in Congress is likely to remain one of arrogance, perhaps no better demonstrated than in Coelho's *Roll Call* interview:

> When I was DCCC [Democratic Congressional Campaign Committee] chairman we undertook an incumbent protection strategy and we lost very few incumbents. I felt very strongly that no incumbent should lose. You have tremendous, tremendous tools you can use that a challenger cannot use.

Stepping back from these policy arguments, however, one sees a deeper issue in the term-limits debate, an issue that takes us to our very foundations as a nation. No one can doubt that America was dedicated to the proposition that each of us is and ought to be free—free to plan and live his own life, as a private individual, under a government instituted to secure that freedom. Thus, implicit in our founding vision is the idea that most human affairs take place in what today we call the private sector. That sector—and this is the crucial point—is primary: government comes from it, not the other way around. When we send men and women to Congress to "represent" us, therefore, we want them to understand that they represent *us*, the overwhelming number of Americans who live our daily lives in that private sector. Moreover, we want them to remember that it is to that private world that they must return, to live under the laws they have made as our representatives. That, in essence, is the message implicit in the growing call for term limits. It is not simply or even primarily a message about "good government." Rather, it is a message about the very place of government in the larger scheme of things. Government is meant to be our servant, to assist us by securing our liberty as we live our essentially private lives. It is not meant to be our master in some grand public adventure.

In this volume we endeavor to provide the reader with thoughtful arguments on both sides of this American debate. We leave it to the reader to determine where the merits of the arguments lie.

2. Term Limits

George F. Will

The Baltimore Orioles, a few years ago, were managed by a Napoleonic figure named Earl Weaver, who was the scourge of American League umpires. One of Weaver's favorite techniques was to run out of the dugout, shove his chin into the chest of a much larger umpire and shout at the top of his lungs, "Are you going to get any better or is this *it*?" The American people looking at government in Washington have decided that *it* isn't getting any better, that this is *it* and that this won't do. They are thinking of Washington and the politics conducted here the way people used to think of the Washington Senators, when they were owned by Clark Griffith, who said one day, "Fans like home runs and we have assembled a pitching staff to please our fans." Term limits have come to remedy what ails government.

I am not going to discuss the politics or the law of term limits. Let me imbue the issue with a larger and more resonating philosophic argument. To the extent that America's intellectual pedigree goes back to John Locke, Americans have been, at best, ambivalent about government. It was Locke who described government as a nuisance necessary to cope with inconveniences, inconveniences being the operative term. Locke said that man is mildly individualistic, mildly social, and altogether a mild creature; government, therefore, has a mild task and is not perhaps as important as other philosophers have said. It is my attempt, and here I depart, I know, from many proponents of term limits, to advocate term limits to restore the good name of government and particularly to restore the good name and supremacy of Congress within our constitutional system.

I take the text for my sermon from Alexander Hamilton, the *Federalist*, no. 68: "The true test of a good government is its aptitude and tendency."[1] The importance of constitutional questions and answers is that proper deliberation defines the tendency of the government.

---

[1]Alexander Hamilton, *Federalist*, no. 68, Jacob E. Cooke, ed. (Middletown, Conn.: Wesleyan University Press, 1961), p. 461.

How did I change my mind on this subject? It was, if this is not an oxymoron, a slow epiphany. It began one day when I was in front of an audience and someone said, "What do you think of term limits?" I said, in the usual Washington way, that I was opposed to them because if we did not have seasoned professionals, we would not have the good government that we've got. At which point I began to rethink. And since then I have come to ask questions about careerism in the context of a government that has shed all the restraints once implicit in the doctrine of enumerated powers.

The Founding Fathers were cognizant of the idea of term limits; term limits existed in the Articles of Confederation. The Founding Fathers, to the extent that they even considered the issue, did consider it necessary to consider it, but then rejected term limits. And the Founding Fathers were, in my judgment, right so to do because term limits are, in fact, an excision from freedom of choice and all such excisions ought to be justified. What justifies them now is the nature of the modern state.

It is not my purpose in advocating term limits to make Congress more responsive to the people; Congress is painfully and excessively responsive to the people. Congress is a hair-trigger seismograph trembling to every organized appetite in the country. My aim with term limits is not to make Congress closer to the people, but to establish a constitutional distance for a more deliberative process, all of which would restore to Congress its proper stature. A deliberative Congress would cut the Presidency down to size from its current swollen nature. This notable growth of the executive is an accident of the post-World War II coincidence of television and the Cold War. Term limits would make Congress bolder, more independent, and less risk-averse. Then Congress would take on more of the issues that it has been only too happy to cede to the judicial branch. Therefore, one consequence, I think, of term limits would be to push the courts back to the margin of American civic life where they belong.

I write as a conservative. Many conservatives are in favor of term limits, which is, in a sense, paradoxical because there are four reasons why conservatives should be rather skeptical. (The scorched-earth conservative, whose aim in life is to discredit government is an exceptional case. He ought to be against term limits because a government operating without term limits is doing a most expeditious job of discrediting itself as we speak.)

16

The four reasons why conservatives might well be suspicious of term limits are, first: All improvements are for the worst; that is why one *is* a conservative. Second: Most reforms, particularly those reaching regime-level questions, as term limits do, have not only unintended consequences, but consequences larger and more complicated than those that were intended. Third: One obvious and certain consequence of term limits is that term limits will end some great careers. Not all long careers are great but all great careers are long. And this is one clear cost which must be acknowledged up front. These careers would be a casualty. And fourth: Conservatives must face the daunting fact that the Founding Fathers did not choose to include term limits in the Constitution.

If we could ask the Founding Fathers if they were concerned about term limits and political careerism, they might return your inquiry with a blank stare. The idea that anyone would want to live in the kind of cities that were going to hold American government—New York or Philadelphia or, soon after, Washington—would have struck them as bizarre. (Almost a century later, Washington had not improved. At the time of Lincoln, the capital had pigs rooting in the mud of Pennsylvania Avenue. It was not a pleasant place.)[2] Indeed, it could be argued that as an alternative to term limits, banning air conditioning would have much the same effect in Washington, I think, by ending the attractiveness and allure of a long career in Congress.

But in the Jeffersonian era those who wanted a long life in politics practiced a kind of musical chairs, serving perhaps in Congress and then going back to, say, the governorship or even the state legislature of Virginia, which to Virginians then and, I think, now does not seem like a step down.

What began to change America was the Civil War, which produced the interventionist state and all the attributes of a modern, industrial, united capitalist economy. It was after the Civil War that the tariff became the dominating political issue in the United States. The tariff issue fueled the career politician in Washington in two ways. The imposition of a tariff conferred a favor which was politically useful as an incumbent-protection device; and the tariff raised money which

[2]Robert V. Remini, *Henry Clay: Statesman for the Union* (New York: W.W. Norton, 1991), p. 45.

could then be spent on another group. So the tariff was a two-fer serving the interests of constant incumbency.

Furthermore, at the turn of the century the world became obsessed with the cult of professionalism. Careerism suited the mood of modernity. Remember, twelve years after the turn of the century the United States elected, as president, a political scientist. In this atmosphere of heightened respect for professionalism, expertise, and science, including the social sciences, we see the rise of careerism in the political class as the embodiment of a presumably necessary professionalism and expertise. This occurred rather late in the American evolution and tended to overshadow the reality of a divided American tradition in thinking about public service.

This divided thinking about the tradition of public service has been revivified by developments in American historiography associated primarily with Bernard Bailyn and Gordon Wood. The research of Bailyn and Wood has enriched our understanding of the sources and the qualities of the American Revolution and the American founding. Properly understood, these gentlemen argue, there is not one strain, as we have often been told, but two mingled strains in the American idea of republican government. The strain with which we are all familiar is the Lockean strain characterized by individualism, natural rights, and limited government in a state of nature that is mildly inconvenient. All that was to be resolved by a social contract to create a government with a not very complicated mandate. Against that is a strain still being unearthed in the pamphlets and literature and rhetoric of the colonial and revolutionary period. This is the strain of classical republicanism, which argues that man is a social creature whose participation in the civic life is essential to his virtue and his happiness. That taps into the Founders' preoccupation with the sociology of virtue in which Alexander Hamilton and Thomas Jefferson were deeply interested.

Jefferson, of course, said, keep your cities in Europe; have an agrarian society; have an expansive society; when in doubt bend the Constitution to make the Louisiana Purchase for that end; because the agrarian society was necessary for the sociology of virtue as Jefferson understood it, a requisite for a free society. Alexander Hamilton came to opposite conclusions with a similar aim. He said that a moneyed society with a free circulation of capital and labor was necessary to dissolve the stratification of an oligarchic southern slavocracy of the sort that he feared would otherwise dominate America. In the thinking and writing of these two people, the polarities of American political argument were struck early.

Today, as we look at the sociology of virtue, what worries us is whether it is encouraged or discouraged by careerism in the context of the modern state with its myriad subsidizing, regulating, organizing activities that permeate American life. Careerism exists in the context of what can best be called supply-side politics. That is to say, we have government programs, not because groups demanded them, but we have government programs in order to create groups that will demand their continuation and elaboration. The honey subsidy, the wool subsidy, and all the rest are fairly well known. In this 20th century celebration of careerism, professionalism, and social science, we have developed a novel, and I think wrong, idea of national social health. Mistakenly, we measure the national social health by the level of government activity. That measure is not correct.

Term limits should not be favored because they will have particular policy outcomes; neither the policy outcomes nor, I think, the advantage to one party or another can be known. In fact, I believe such outcomes and advantages will be negligible. I would not say, for example, that term limits would result in decreased federal spending. Indeed, it is arguable that if term limits have the consequence that I anticipate they would have, which is to rehabilitate the good name of Congress and deepen public trust of our institutions, they would dissolve the distrust that underlies the only strong passion which currently unites Americans—taxophobia. Therefore one result may be a more energetic federal government. I don't know and frankly I don't care. What I do know is that no one seriously defends Congress's current pattern of activity, which is indiscriminate in its use of federal power and responsive only to the most basic, narrowest, and most parochial motives.

Now it is very clear that what we have today is a system of running for office among the career political class that is perhaps the most pure form of entrepreneurship in the United States. The political entrepreneur finds a market, a district, and a market niche within that district. He attracts the venture capital of investors called campaign contributors, who help him merchandise himself on the basis of market research and who hope to get a return on their investment if he wins.

That is not an elegant or happy picture. Some people say that what we need to take care of the defects of political entrepreneurship is campaign finance reform. I will not go into that as an alternative to term limits other than to say that all campaign finance reform turns in the end to limits on spending and giving. This strikes me as facially unconstitutional: government would be rationing the permissible amount of political speech.

A desirable institutional outcome of term limits is, as I intimated earlier, to establish Congress to be what the Founding Fathers intended: the first branch of government. It is in article I of the Constitution; it sits symbolically on the Hill where four quadrants of the federal city meet. Congress should be, it seems to me, the dominant branch of government, but it has been eclipsed by the executive in the 20th century, particularly since the late 1940s, with the arrival of the Cold War and television, which made the Presidency prominent and encouraged Americans to confuse prominence with power.

In fact, the Presidency is an inherently weak office, by which I mean the executive is constitutionally weak; there is very little a President can do on his own. And indeed, there was very little Presidents tried to do on their own until Teddy Roosevelt, the inventor of the rhetoric of the Presidency. I am deeply indebted to a wonderful book by Jeffrey Tulis of the University of Texas, published by Princeton. *The Rhetorical Presidency* describes the evolution of the President understood today as the nation's agenda writer and moral tutor. Ever since Teddy Roosevelt went campaigning for the Hepburn Act, the Presidency has become a constant presence in the American mind. This watery Caesarism is a modern invention and, I think, a departure from the proper constitutional balance. Of course, it is well known that between Thomas Jefferson and Woodrow Wilson, not one president even went to the Congress to deliver, rhetorically, a State-of-the-Union address. Throughout the 19th century the principal presidential communications were in writing to the legislative branch and not written to the people. What has developed since then is an idea of the President as the nation's moral tutor.

One very fascinating fact about our Presidency is that the office is a hostage to the attributes of its occupant. The office of prime minister of Great Britain was essentially the same in its powers under Clement Attlee or Margaret Thatcher. The real effective powers of the Presidency vary radically with the attributes of the men who hold it. Think of Jimmy Carter in the summer of 1979 and Ronald Reagan two years later in the summer of 1981 and you see a transformed office. This transformation means that the office is a sometime thing and that it is not a reliable anchor for the government of a great nation.

When Teddy Roosevelt campaigned for the Hepburn Act, he thought the issue of railroad regulation to be a regime-level question, important for preventing class division in this country. So important did he think this issue that it justified what he understood to be a departure from the constitutional understanding of the role of the President.

Woodrow Wilson was the first President to criticize the Founding Fathers. He really set the agenda for the progressives and New Dealers who said that the Founding Fathers' intentions were all very well in their day but were no longer apposite to a country such as ours. Wilson said it was the duty of the President to inspirit the people; the president's job was the interpretation of the inchoate and unexpressed and inarticulate views of the country. This plebiscitary understanding of the Presidency was novel and subverted the genius of the Constitution, which is a structure of indirection that was to produce a deliberative body in the Congress of the United States. Congress, being the locus of popular sovereignty in the United States, is the locus of the modern political problem.

The old political problem debated for literally several millennia was the problem of the ruler versus the ruled. As the modern age began, the old problem was thought to have been solved by popular sovereignty, which would make the ruled the masters of the rulers. This turns out not to be quite that simple because the sovereign people themselves can be a problem. And it was Alexis de Tocqueville in this country, looking at popular sovereignty, who said that we needed to worry about a government that could degrade people without tormenting them. It was Tocqueville who raised the possibility that a solicitous, kindly government could, by its hyperactivity, inflame appetites and produce the kind of avaricious grasping factionalism that, combined with a weakening of restraints on the federal government's sense of its proper sphere, would produce something like what we have today, a maelstrom of interests hoping against hope with some kind of Cuisinart™ theory of the public interest that whatever happens from the public churning, whatever puree comes out at the end of the day, shall be called the national interest. Well, it is not adequate. No one is happy with what we have today.

Ever since Plato began the Western tradition of political thought, philosophers have worried about the decay of good regimes. Plato said that if you didn't take the right math courses everything went bad. Shakespeare said, "Untune that string, take but degree away and hark what discord follows."[3] Gibbon focused attention on the collapse of Rome and made it a permanent theme in Western political thought. The problem of decay is one of particular poignancy in the United States because we had a founding moment to be viewed not just through the rosy spectacle of national nostalgia, but to be seen realistically as a golden age of statecraft. It is now through the issue of term limits that the American people are coming to grips with an old argument: constitutions encourage a certain kind of behavior and that behavior has a shaping effect on individual character and the character of the polity. I once wrote a book, read by dozens, called *Statecraft As Soulcraft*; the subtitle was "What Government Does," not "What Government Should Do." The theme was that government, by the way it functions, by its institutions, by the values it encourages and discourages in its routine behavior cannot help but affect the soul of the citizenry.

Those who favor term limits for the reason that I do, do so because we believe that by changing the sociology of the electorate we can change the motives that people have for coming into government. We are more apt to produce a calm, reasonable, civil, detached, and less risk-averse Congress. Virtue, we think, is not natural but nurtured; it is a product of artifice, and term limits are an artifice that will produce something like the kind of virtues that Madison talked about in the *Federalist*, no. 10, when he said, "It is the duty of public institutions to refine and enlarge public opinion, to add reason to willfulness."[4] Term limitation, of course, is not a silver bullet; it is not an attempt to make something straight from the crooked timber of humanity. On the contrary, it is a hard-headed Madisonian reform. It is an attempt to change the structure of

[3]William Shakespeare, *Troilus and Cressida*, 1, 3, 109.

[4]James Madison, the *Federalist*, no. 10, Jacob E. Cooke, ed. (Middletown, Conn.: Wesleyan University Press, 1961), p. 62.

government to accommodate the timeless human motive and the changing nature of the modern state.

To those who argue that term limitation is anti-democratic, I say that the United States has never flirted for a minute with untrameled majoritarianism. The first Congress, you may recall, passed the First Amendment which begins, Congress, the popular branch of government, "shall make no law" regarding this, that, and the other thing. Limits on the willfulness and choice of the electorate are not new. It does seem to me that the American people get what they want if they want it steadily, intensely, and over time. Today the numbers are encouraging for the advocates of term limits because it seems clear that as more localities, city councils, states, and state legislatures impose term limits, Congress, by refusing to debate the issue and send it to the states for deliberation, stands forth as drained of its legitimacy in a nation that clearly prefers some other outcome than the one Congress is willing to permit. It is my belief, as someone who loves Washington and loves politics and the federal government, that term limits can restore some of the brio to politics that has been lost. When Barry Goldwater, for whom I cast my first presidential vote, went into politics in 1952, he said to a friend, "Well, it ain't for life and it might be fun." It is that spirit which term limits might return to government.

PART II

THE POLITICS OF TERM LIMITS

3. From the Voters with Care

Paul Jacob

The American people want term limits for members of Congress as well as for virtually every person serving in elective office. That desire is strong and consistent as demonstrated by national polls and election results in seventeen states and hundreds of cities and counties across the country (see Figure 1).[1] Seventeen states have passed congressional and/or state legislative term-limits laws overwhelmingly. The margin of victory in those elections was on average 2 to 1, with the victory percentage going as high as 77 percent in both Florida and Wyoming. In the last year, voters in the nation's two largest cities—New York and Los Angeles—limited terms for city officials.[2]

I want to thank Norman Leahy, Director of Research at U.S. Term Limits, for his help in gathering information for this paper.

[1]Term limits have won in every state they have been on the ballot and in virtually every one of the hundreds of cities, counties, and other jurisdictions where citizens have had a chance to vote on the issue. Bill McAllister, "Term-Limit Initiatives Win Overwhelming Support of State Voters," *Washington Post*, November 4, 1992, p. A31; Bruce Frankel, "Term Limits to Be Among Clinton's First Challenges," *USA Today*, November 5, 1992, p. 13A. Survey of various Secretaries of State and State Election Boards by U.S. Term Limits. Daniel B. Wood, "Populist Revolt Rolls On As Voters Across the US Approve Term Limits," *Christian Science Monitor*, November 4, 1993, p. 2; Erica Gould, "The Municipal Term Limits Groundswell," U.S. Term Limits Foundation, *Outlook Series*, Vol. 2, No. 3, August 1993, p. 1.

Polls have consistently put support for term limits on Congress at between 75 and 80 percent with some polls showing support as high as 86 percent. Fabrizio, McLaughlin & Associates' poll commissioned by U.S. Term Limits—a survey of 1,000 adults conducted between May 20 and May 23, 1993, with accuracy of ±3.1 percent at the 95 percent confidence interval. Bob Bernick, Jr., "Most Utahns Favor Term Limits," *Deseret News*, August 29, 1993—*Deseret News*/KSL poll conducted by Dan Jones & Associates, August 3–5, 1993, of 600 adults with an error margin of ±4 percent. National Taxpayers Union Foundation poll, *Capitol Ideas*, Vol. 1, No. 1, Sept./Oct. 1992. *Wall Street Journal*/NBC News poll; *Wall Street Journal*, April 17, 1992, p. A12.

[2]Marc Lacey, "Wish For Council Term Limits Clear—Impact Less Certain," *Los Angeles Times*, April 22, 1993, p. B13; Steven Lee Myers, "New Yorkers Approve Limit of 2 Terms for City Officials," *New York Times*, November 3, 1993, p. B1.

Figure 1
1992 TERM LIMIT BALLOT RESULTS

State	Yes (%)	Votes	No (%)	Votes
Arizona	74	1,026,830	26	356,799
Arkansas	60	494,326	40	330,836
California	64	6,578,637	36	3,769,511
Colorado	71	652,322	29	269,831
Florida	77	3,625,500	23	1,097,127
Michigan	59	2,323,171	41	1,629,368
Missouri	74	1,590,552	26	558,299
Montana	67	264,174	33	130,695
Nebraska	68	481,048	32	224,114
N. Dakota	56	162,150	44	129,930
Ohio	66	2,897,054	34	1,476,436
Oregon	70	1,003,706	30	439,694
S. Dakota	64	205,074	36	117,702
Washington	52	1,119,985	48	1,018,260
Wyoming	77	150,113	23	44,424
Average/Total:	**66%**	**22,574,642**	**34%**	**11,593,026**

Polls have consistently shown support for a constitutional amendment for uniform congressional term limits to be between 75 and 80 percent.[3] The incredible aspect of the polling is that support for term limits shows almost no demographic variation.[4] People of all races, both major parties, all political philosophies, both genders, and all ages favor limiting terms. A May 1993 survey by Fabrizio, McLaughlin & Associates showed 75 percent of Democrats favor limits, 76 percent of Independents, and 79 percent of Republicans.

Opponents concede that the voters are strongly in favor of term limits, but then are quick to add that just because the people support an idea does not make it a good idea.[5] Their enthusiasm in making this latter point, I believe, underscores a strong disdain for the very people government is supposed to be serving. In the private economy, a producer of a product could likewise claim that whether or

[3]See note 1.

[4]John H. Fund, "Term Limitations: An Idea Whose Time Has Come," *Cato Institute Policy Analysis* 141, October 30, 1990.

[5]Testimony by Norman J. Ornstein before the House Judiciary Subcommittee on Civil and Constitutional Rights, November 18, 1993, p. 1.

not consumers purchase the product has no bearing on whether it is a "good product." But unless that producer changes to fit what is "popular," he or she will soon be out of business. Likewise, government has no legitimacy if it ignores the will of the people. Barring an abridgement of the fundamental rights of citizens upon which our American government was instituted—i.e. life, liberty, and pursuit of happiness—government should function and be structured precisely as the majority feels will be most beneficial.

Congressional term limitations are also portrayed by opponents as nothing more than blind citizen anger fueled by scandals like the House bank fiasco. Debbie Dingell, the wife of Representative John Dingell (D-Mich.) and organizer of the opposition campaign in Michigan, referred to term-limits activists as "frustrated children."[6] That attitude not only displays the kind of arrogance citizens are seeking to curb; it also ignores the fact that the success of term limits at the local level is driven most often by a desire to rejuvenate citizen participation and is not tied to any scandal or corruption. Term-limitation laws have been passed by the voters, again with usually overwhelming majorities, in major cities including New York, Los Angeles, Cincinnati, San Francisco, Houston, Kansas City, San Antonio, and New Orleans.[7] Vast support for existing term limits on the President and 37 state governors demonstrates that support for term limits has much less to do with voter anger and more to do with the fact that the voters believe regular rotation in office is sound public policy.[8]

What are the public policy implications of congressional term limits? Why does such a significant majority of citizens want term limits? Who opposes term limits and why do they oppose them? What will be the effect of term limits?

People support term limits to accomplish two primary goals: (1) rejuvenate the election process and (2) restore a citizen legislature.[9]

[6]Dawson Bell, "Lawmakers Rap Term Limit Idea," *Detroit Free Press*, May 30, 1992.

[7]Erica Gould, "The Municipal Term Limits Groundswell," U.S. Term Limits Foundation, *Outlook Series*, Vol. 2, No. 3, August 1993, p. 2.

[8]Bernick, p. A7.

[9]Numerous reasons can be found for people to support term limits, but the two main reasons articulated by key advocates center on the lack of meaningful and competitive elections and the need for legislators to view themselves as citizen-lawmakers, not career politicians. "Our democracy is in danger because elections have become the closest thing to being rigged: they are, for the most part, lifeless, ideologically hollow show elections with gerrymandered districts, voter indifference,

Let's examine what problems currently exist in these two areas and what effect term limits could have.

The Election System

The present system is marked by a tremendous reelection rate for incumbents. In 1988, incumbents who sought reelection were returned to Congress 96 percent of the time. In 1990, the reelection rate was 98 percent with 74 congressmen drawing no major party opponent. In 1992, the House bank scandal combined with increasing gridlock to push out some of the most respected members of Congress with some of the least respected. Still the reelection rate was 93 percent.[10]

Why do so many congressmen win reelection? The answer is fairly simple: Incumbents have all the advantages. Incumbent advantages include both those naturally occurring and those that congressmen have voted to bestow upon themselves.

The Franking Privilege. The franking privilege allows members of Congress to send mail to their constituents at taxpayer expense touting the work the congressman has been doing. In fact, last year members were able to send mail to voters outside their congressional districts to prepare for redistricting.[11] There can be no more blatant sign that these mailings are oriented for reelection purposes, as opposed to educational purposes, than letting them be sent to people who are presently *not* constituents, but future voters. In order to get a sense of the impact of that free mail on an election campaign, it is important to understand that the average incumbent spends more of the taxpayers' money on franked mailings than the average challenger spends on his entire campaign.[12] Congressmen could vote to

---

and absurdly high reelection rates," writes Edward H. Crane, "Reclaiming the Political Process," *Market Liberalism* (Washington, D.C.: Cato Institute, 1993). Bill McAllister, "Term-Limit Initiatives Win Overwhelming Support of State Voters," *Washington Post*, November 4, 1992, p. A31; James K. Coyne and John H. Fund, *Cleaning House: America's Campaign for Term Limits* (Washington, D.C.: Regnery Gateway, 1992), pp. 58–59. Mark Petracca, "The Poison of Professional Politics," Cato Institute, Policy Analysis 151, May 10, 1991. Roger E. Meiners and Roger LeRoy Miller, *Gridlock in Government: How to Break the Stagnation of America* (Washington, D.C.: Free Congress Foundation, 1992).

[10]"1992 Election Results & Analysis," *Congressional Monitor*, November 5, 1992, p. 17.

[11]Coyne and Fund, pp. 58–59.

[12]Ibid.

put an end to unsolicited franked mail, but they have steadfastly refused to do so because it would make their careers in Congress less secure.

Congressional Staff. Members of Congress average 22 staff members and more than one office per district.[13] Those staffers work not only on legislative business, but also on constituent services—which amounts to helping cut through the very red tape that members of Congress have created or allowed to exist—and public relations. Staff, public employees, are charged with getting the congressman's name in the paper or picture on television, as well as putting the right "spin" on news. Constituent services and public relations win votes for the reelection of the congressman while the taxpayers foot the bill.

Sometimes the use of staff for campaign purposes is even more blatant. Trudy Pearce writes in *Cleaning Up Congress:*

> Many legislators have found ways to encourage some of their congressional staffers to become campaign staffers. Staffers can take "leave without pay" for a month or so to go work the legislator's campaign. During this time they still receive their health and life insurance benefits and can still build their pension benefits. They simply do not get their paycheck for that period of time. But calling this absence "leave without pay" is somewhat deceiving. By using temporary pay increases before and/or after the leave, legislators, in effect pay the staffers for the campaign work with our tax money.[14]

Media Advantages. Though the politicians in Washington, D.C., have built themselves a TV and radio studio at taxpayers' expense,[15] the incumbents' main advantage in garnering media attention accrues naturally. Because a member of Congress represents approximately 575,000 people, what a congressman says or does is news and receives a great deal of coverage—as it should. Challengers simply cannot expect to receive the same degree of media attention. The dilemma for our system is that without significant news coverage of a challenger, voters opposing the incumbent may stay home,

---

[13]Ibid., pp. 101-2.

[14]Trudy Pearce, *Cleaning Up Congress* (Washington, D.C.: Citizens for Congressional Reform, 1991), p. 33.

[15]Coyne and Fund, p. 14.

or if they do vote, decide not to vote for someone about whom they feel they are not fully informed. Some suggest mandating coverage, but this creates potential First Amendment problems and it may be almost impossible to truly equalize coverage.

Campaign Finance Rules. The rules governing the financing of campaigns are passed by members of Congress. It is little wonder then that the rules, no matter how often they are changed, continue to benefit incumbents and hurt challengers. The recent bills passed by the House and the Senate demonstrate the same tendency for incumbents to rig campaign finance laws in order to protect themselves from competition.

Political Action Committees (PACs) give over 90 percent of their funding to incumbents.[16] Could that be why PACs have been allowed by Congress to give five times as much money to campaigns as an individual can? Though there is public support for abolishing PACs, H.R. 3 passed by the House doesn't touch them because many House members are dependent on PAC funding.

In fact, the legislation actually locks in a very major role for PACs by creating a system whereby each candidate can only raise $600,000 with one-third required to come from PACs.[17] This campaign finance scheme effectively ensures an incumbent will have a 3-to-2 spending advantage over the challenger in all but the rarest of campaigns, because PACs give over 90 percent of their funds to incumbents. Not to mention that because incumbents have the power to vote on the spending of $1.5 trillion dollars annually, they have an incredible advantage in raising funds not only from PACs, but also from individuals who want to gain access or influence.

What the House campaign finance bill does include is also revealing. It includes public financing even though voter surveys strongly show Americans oppose having taxpayers pick up the bill for congressional campaigns.[18] The legislation includes spending caps, which many believe adversely impact challengers who often must outspend incumbents to make up for the numerous other advantages incumbents enjoy.[19]

[16]Federal Election Commission, "1992 Congressional Election Spending Jumps 52% to $678 Million," FEC, March 4, 1993.

[17]H.R. 3, Title II, section 201, 103rd Congress, 1st Session.

[18]Fabrizio, McLaughlin & Associates poll.

[19]H.R. 3, Title II, section 201, 103rd Congress, 1st Session.

But worst of all, the House bill includes protections for incumbents from those they fear most: organized voters. The House's so-called reform would give additional taxpayer money to incumbents when voters independently spend money against them.[20] This measure seems designed to stop an individual (like Ross Perot) or an organized group from being able to negatively impact an incumbent.

Furthermore, the House bill would require that any advocacy organization that lobbies Congress report all its contributors to Congress.[21] The purpose is clear: To intimidate any donor supporting an organization whose purpose might be against the interests of the careerists in control of Congress.

While most Americans strongly favor campaign finance reforms, Congress not only refuses to enact real reforms, but arrogantly uses campaign finance legislation as a ruse to try to push citizen groups out of the election process and to further their own advantages— all the while pretending to selflessly reform the system. Dwight R. Lee points out that incumbent congressmen are unlikely to pass any real campaign finance reform because it would necessarily reduce their personal power. Yet, reform that evens the playing field can come from term limits, says Lee, because "term limits would directly and effectively accomplish what campaign finance reform never will—a significant reduction in the ability of incumbents to perpetuate themselves in office."[22]

Term limits will not directly change or diminish all incumbent advantages. However, limits will prevent incumbents from parlaying these advantages into a lifetime career in Congress. Term limitation creates open seats where experience shows the races and the campaign funding are much more competitive. The vast majority of women and minorities in Congress today have not defeated long-time incumbents, but won in open-seat races.

A former congressional staffer and the author of *Hill Rat*, John Jackley wrote about the reelection power of incumbents:

> The advantages of today's House incumbents are so great that many political scientists refuse to analyze their campaigns. Writing in *Congress and the Presidency*, Susan Welch

[20]H.R. 3, Title I, section 604, 103rd Congress, 1st Session.

[21]H.R. 3, Title VI, section 324, 103rd Congress, 1st Session.

[22]Dwight R. Lee, "Fiscal Pollution and the Case for Congressional Term Limits," Center for the Study of American Business, Washington University—St. Louis, *Contemporary Issues Series*, No. 51, April 1992, p. 12.

noted that races with incumbents were not part of her research because "it is only through open seats that major changes in the composition of Congress will occur."[23]

Furthermore, a new Congress of citizen-legislators who cannot have a lifelong political career will no longer have their own self-interest standing in the way of necessary reforms. That is why supporters argue that term limits will open the door to a plethora of reforms. Congressmen today are largely careerist, giving them a personal interest in keeping the numerous election advantages they enjoy in order to make their careers more secure. By contrast congressmen under term limits will not be able to make a career out of service in Congress, removing the inclination to interfere with campaign reforms or other institutional reforms.

A Citizen Legislature

Though cynical Washington, D.C., insiders argue that it is not achievable, the American people deeply believe in a citizen legislature. The concept that people in public office should be "of the people," as Lincoln said, serving the public for a short period of time, as opposed to professionals pursuing their own careers, is part of the American democratic experience.

Ed Crane, president of the Cato Institute, observes: "What I would like to see is a return to the citizen legislatures envisioned by the Founders of this nation who, I believe, would have been appalled at the idea of professional politicians, of professional legislators."[24]

Our nation's Founders were not the first to recognize rotation in office as an important ingredient of representative democracy. Term limits were part of the democratic system in ancient Athens. Aristotle believed that rotation in office was a crucial principle of representative democracy, the idea of "ruling and being ruled in turn."[25] The great Roman Cicero also praised rotation in office.[26]

---

[23]John L. Jackley, *Hill Rat: Blowing the Lid Off Congress* (Washington, D.C.: Regnery Gateway, 1992), p. 25. Susan Welch, "Congressional Nomination Procedures and the Representation of Women," *Congress and the Presidency*, Vol. 16 (Autumn 1989).

[24]Edward H. Crane, "Term Limits for a Citizen Legislature," *Vital Speeches*, Vol. LVII, No. 5, December 15, 1990, p. 148.

[25]Mark P. Petracca, "Rotation in Office: The History of an Idea," *Limiting Legislative Terms*, ed. Gerald Benjamin and Michael J. Malbin (Washington, D.C.: C.Q. Press, 1992), pp. 19–51.

[26]Ibid.

The danger of the corrupting influence of long service in public office was well understood by our Founders as well as other great American leaders. George Washington stepped down after two terms and established a tradition contrary to lifetime tenure. Thomas Jefferson's critique of the Constitution argued that it lacked two essential elements—a bill of rights and a provision for mandatory rotation in office. He wrote, "Whenever a man has cast a longing eye on them [offices], a rottenness begins in his conduct."[27]

Abraham Lincoln stepped down after one term in Congress as was the custom in his congressional district. As President, he stated:

> If our American society and United States Government are overthrown, it will come from the voracious desire for office, this wriggle to live without toil, work, and labor—from which I am not free myself.[28]

Ed Crane points out what many people today believe: "The less time a member of Congress spends in Washington, D.C., the less chance there is for that insidious process of corruption to occur."[29]

Congress's antagonism toward mandatory rotation in office and the average members' strong desire to make a career of serving in the institution is evident. But the issue of passing laws for the mass of citizens that do not apply to Congress may be the most egregious strike by Congress against the concept of citizen-legislators. As James Madison stated:

> It is a sound and important principle that the representative ought to be acquainted with the interests and circumstances of his constituents. But this principle can extend no further than to those circumstances and interests to which the authority and case of the representative relate . . . That [representatives] can make no law which will not have its full operation on themselves and their friends, as well as on the great mass of society. . . .[30]

---

[27]Lally Weymouth, ed. *Thomas Jefferson: The Man, His World, His Influence* (New York: G.P. Putnam's Sons, 1973).

[28]Mike Klein, "Limiting Congressional Terms: An Historical Perspective," Americans to Limit Congressional Terms, 1990, p. 6.

[29]Edward H. Crane, "Six and Twelve: The Case for Serious Term Limits," *National Civic Review* (Summer 1991), p. 253.

[30]Petracca, "The Poison of Professional Politics," p. 9.

Our Congress has exempted itself from countless laws that the mass of society must obey. These include sexual harassment laws, fairness in employment, worker safety regulations, and others. Is not something wrong with congressmen enjoying one of the most lavish pension systems in the world and then voting on the Social Security retirement benefits of others? It will be interesting to see if members of Congress, as well as federal workers, will propose to receive the same medical benefits and costs as the general public under any new health care law. Presently, their medical plan is far superior to the average American's.[31]

Many citizens feel politicians, especially those in Congress, are out of touch with their life experiences. As George Will has written:

> Many Americans wish that a lot of legislators had a better sense of American life, and particularly of what it is like to be on the receiving end of the high-minded laws and regulations that gush like a cataract from Washington. Term limits, guaranteeing a steady rotation of offices, would help. They would make it impossible for anyone to come to Congress counting on a long career there. Therefore term limits would increase the likelihood that people would come to Congress from established careers, with significant experience in the private sector. Furthermore, term limits would increase the likelihood that people who come to Congress would anticipate returning to the careers in the private sector and therefore would, as they legislate, think about what it is like to live under the laws they make.[32]

A striking example of the disconnectedness of Congress comes from the statement of Senator George McGovern who, after retiring from 24 years in the U.S. Senate, went into a business venture that failed. McGovern commented, "I wish that someone had told me about the problems of running a business. I have to pay taxes, meet a payroll—I wish I had had a better sense of what it took to do that

---

[31]Karen Foerstel, "Members Resist Killing Hill's Health Care Plan," *Roll Call*, November 11, 1993, p. 10 ("The FEHBP (Federal Employees Health Benefit Program) is considered one of the most generous health care programs now in existence. . . ."). Rep. John Myers (R-Ind) said: "It seems you're going to be dragging the federal employees' programs down. Why in the world are you dragging them into this thing [Clinton's proposed national health care plan]?" Quoted in ibid.

[32]George F. Will, *Restoration: Congress, Term Limits and the Recovery of Deliberative Democracy* (New York: The Free Press, 1992), p. 200.

when I was in Washington."[33] Citizen legislators would necessarily have experiences outside of campaigning for and serving in elected office. They would thereby be more connected to and representative of their constituents.

The danger of professional politicians' using the power of their offices to remain in office and for a separate political class to form is significant and alarming. Yet, the citizen-legislator is not merely the absence of the negative career politician but a positive force in its own right. Citizen participation is essential to our system of government. As Madeleine Kunin, the former Democratic governor of Vermont, wrote in the *Los Angeles Times*:

> Breaking the gridlock of incumbency could throw the doors
> wide open to new people and new ideas that would make
> politics rewarding, meaningful, even fun.[34]

Citizens coming to Washington to serve for no more than six years in the U.S. House or one or two terms in the U.S. Senate[35] knowing from the very first day in the Capitol that soon they will return to private station to live under the laws they have made: That is the goal of term limits. It means replacing a system that is closed to the people with an open system encouraging new participants. It means replacing the attitude of "what's in it for me" with "what's best for the country." It won't usher in an age of perfect government, but

[33]John H. Fund, "Making the Case for Term Limits," *Chicago Tribune*, December 16, 1990, p. 3.

[34]Madeleine Kunin, "Term limits Would Rejuvenate Politics," *Los Angeles Times*, September 13, 1991, p. B7.

[35]All state initiatives that include congressional limits have limited Senate terms to two (12 years), but vary on the terms in the House with three terms (6 years) in most states. House limits are: Arizona—6 years; Arkansas—6 years; California—6 years; Colorado—12 years; Florida—8 years; Michigan—6 years; Missouri—8 years; Montana—6 years; Nebraska—8 years; North Dakota—12 years; Ohio—8 years; Oregon—6 years; South Dakota—12 years; Washington—6 years; Wyoming—6 years. Bill McAllister, "Term-Limit Initiatives Win Overwhelming Support of State Voters," *Washington Post*, November 4, 1992, p. A31. House Joint Resolution 160, 103rd Congress, 1st Session, Susan B. Glasser, "With Term-Limiters' Support, Inglis Offers Measure to Restrict Hill Tenure to Six Years," *Roll Call*, March 25, 1993. Ed Crane, president of the Cato Institute, argues: "In order for the concept of a citizen legislature to have meaning, it is imperative that those serving view their time in office as a leave of absence from their real jobs or careers. . . . Two, four or six years is a leave of absence. Twelve years is a career." Crane, "Six and Twelve," pp. 253–54.

it will serve to change the incentive system in Congress—as limits are already doing at the state and local level.

Finally, support for a citizen legislature runs counter to the seniority system now at work in Congress whereby some members gain disproportionate power simply by staying in office longer and longer. Term limits will end this seniority system. Thomas Mann, a political scientist with the Brookings Institution who opposes limits, was quoted as saying, "The seniority system makes no sense in a body that has term limits."[36] I agree. In fact, the seniority system makes no sense—period. Term limits, especially short limits of three terms (six years) in the U.S. House, will mean a swift return to a system of picking committee chairs on the basis of merit, not longevity.

Opponents of Term Limits

Who opposes term limits for members of Congress? The members themselves are the main opponents, but are joined by many major corporations (usually those heavily regulated by the federal government), labor union officials, Common Cause, the League of Women Voters, congressional staffers, lobbyists, and public employees.

A look at the campaign finance reports in state term-limits initiatives or at who is suing to overturn the votes in favor of limits reveals a list of opponents that reads like a who's who of special interests and the insiders of the political system. Campaigns against the state term-limits initiatives have been funded by the liquor lobby, tobacco lobby, drug companies, and those special interests mentioned above—one of which, the League of Women Voters, receives government funding.[37]

It is a sign of the overwhelming support of term limits among the public and the opposition of special interests that term-limits opponents have never been able to sustain an organization or to gain the financial support of any significant number of private citizens. Most campaigns in opposition to limits have had less than a dozen individual contributors. Virtually every penny spent against term

[36]Janet Hook, "Some in Congress Expect Jump-Start with Term Limits," *Washington Times*, November 1, 1993, p. A4.

[37]League of Women Voters Education Fund, "Annual Report FY 1991," League of Women Voters, 1991, pp. 8–10.

limits has been from politicians and special interests.[38] *Common Cause* magazine reported, "Indeed, the contributor report for 'No on 573,' a coalition formed to oppose Washington state's term limits, includes some of the nation's most well-financed lobbying interests: tobacco giants Philip Morris and RJR Nabisco, defense contractors Northrop and General Electric, five labor unions, and the National Rifle Association."[39] It is ironic that the opposition to term limits among politicians and special interests crosses all political lines in the very same way that mass support is evenly found across the political spectrum.

Why do politicians and the organizations mentioned above oppose term limits? They may feel term limits will be bad public policy or will reduce their power and influence. Politicians seeking a career in Congress, or other public office, clearly see term limits as an obstacle to their personal career plans. Victor Kamber, a consultant to organized labor and one of the most vocal opponents of term limits, said recently that organized labor's political strength "is far greater than our numbers."[40] This could explain the opposition of labor leaders to term limits—the resultant turnover might make it increasingly difficult for organized labor to maintain power in excess of its numbers. Yet, rather than attempt to explain the motives of term-limits opponents, an exercise I'm certain they would prefer I not be assigned to perform, I will instead address their arguments against the proposal to limit terms.

One of the major arguments advanced by term-limits opponents is that term limitations are anti-democratic. The opponents' supposed love of democracy is pretty disingenuous when one considers the fact that politicians, the League of Women Voters, Common Cause, and others have regularly and unsuccessfully sued to prevent the people from having an opportunity to vote on term limits. Opponents have also charged that the ultimate aim of the term-limits reformers is a plebiscitary democracy—heady stuff for supposedly antidemocratic interests.

[38]Information taken from Washington Public Disclosure Commission report of "No on 573" and "No on 553"; Arkansas secretary of state's office, Campaign Finance reports of "Arkansans for Representative Democracy" (opposed to Amendment 4); Michigan Bureau of Elections reports of "Michigan Citizens Committee Against Term Limitation" and "Michigan Citizens Alert."

[39]Amy E. Young, "The Money Behind the Movement," *Common Cause*, Summer 1993, p. 39.

[40]Victor Kamber, *Newsmaker Sunday*, CNN, October 17, 1993.

The truth is that term limiters hope to advance the straightforward cause of more competitive elections and democracy in the structuring of government. Term limits in California were largely credited with a significant number of incumbents seeking other public office or retiring in 1992. The resultant open-seat elections caused a 50 percent increase in the number of candidates in legislative races.[41] That simply means more choices for the voters. Ending the near-monopoly control of public office opens the system to new people, and more people, which enlivens democracy.

The curious part of the argument made by term-limits opponents is that they seem to favor democracy only in the narrow confines of candidate races under the present system which is universally condemned as unfair. Term limiters believe in a more robust and meaningful democracy not limited to simply choosing between candidate A and candidate B, but able to impact the functions and structure of government. It is nothing short of absurd to call a movement antidemocratic that has collected the signatures of close to four million Americans, fought off legal challenges to be able to allow their fellow citizens to cast ballots, and won the overwhelming vote in countless elections. The actions of the citizen activists in the term-limits movement are democracy at its finest.

Opponents argue that experience is necessary to run a complex government. But one only has to point to the savings-and-loan debacle or the $4 trillion national debt to demonstrate that the experience of the most experienced Congresses in American history was the problem, not the solution. Limit proponents argue that we need people experienced in what has become known as "the real world," the nongovernment sector of the economy. Americans embrace term limits precisely because they have faith, not in the knowledge of experts, but in the common sense of their fellow citizens.

Finally, adversaries claim that term limits on Congress will only shift power from elected officials to unselected bureaucrats, congressional staffers, and lobbyists. It may be enough evidence to the contrary that a 1992 Gallup poll showed all of these groups oppose term limits.[42] Lobbyists have filed suit in Florida to overturn the

[41]Norman Leahy, "Expanding Democracy," U.S. Term Limits Foundation, *Outlook Series*, Vol. 1, No. 5, August 1992.

[42]Gallup Poll, September 1992, "Attitudes Toward Proposed Policy Changes for Members of Congress," conducted for Center for Independent Thought.

successful term-limits amendment. A congressional staffer is part of the lawsuit now before a federal court in Washington state. The public employees' unions in Washington state, Michigan, and elsewhere have contributed financially against term-limits initiatives and even served as headquarters for the opposition campaigns.

The rise in tenure of members of Congress has seen a corresponding rise in the size and power of the bureaucracy, the staff, and lobbyists. Lobbyists depend on long-term relationships that term limits will take away. The staff clearly gains power as members stay in office over long periods of time. The bureaucracy also gains from those serving longer in Congress, because, according to a National Taxpayers Union study, the longer a member of Congress serves the more likely he is to vote for increased spending.[43]

Do Term Limits Work?

Perhaps the most important question of all is: Will term limits work? Because none of the measures passed by voters at the state level have yet required anyone to step down and only a relatively few local term-limits laws have gone into effect, there is little empirical evidence. However, what evidence does exist, mainly anecdotal, points to the success of term limits.

A study of the considerable experience of term limits on gubernatorial elections by John Armor, author and constitutional lawyer, shows that gubernatorial elections in term-limited states are more competitive than in nonlimited states. That is true not only in the open-seat elections created by a governor's having to step down, but also in the election cycle where a governor can run for re-election.[44] Knowing an open seat is approaching in the future seems to encourage candidates to run aggressive campaigns in order to increase their name recognition for the future, even if they don't win at that particular election. And sometimes they do win. There is every reason to believe that the same dynamic will take place in congressional elections.

In California, where Proposition 140 passed in 1990 limiting the state's assemblymen to six years in office, a large number of careerists have already left, allowing 27 freshmen to go to Sacramento

---

[43]James L. Payne, *The Culture of Spending* (San Francisco: ICS Press, 1991), p. 80.

[44]John Armor, "Term Limits Work: Fifty Years in the Election of State Governors," U.S. Term Limits Foundation, *Outlook Series*, Vol. 2, No. 4, October 1993.

in 1993. Those persons include more women and minorities and people from all walks of life—precisely the kind of citizen-legislators term-limits advocates desire. As Jerry Gillam reported in the *Los Angeles Times:*

> Among the 27 [freshmen legislators] are a former U.S. Air Force pilot, a former sheriff-coroner, a paralegal, a retired teacher, a video store owner, a businesswoman-homemaker, a children's advocate, an interior designer, a retired sheriff's lieutenant, and a number of businessmen, lawyers and former City Council members.[45]

The result of all those new citizen-legislators was a less partisan session and the first state budget passed on time in recent memory.

Henry Lyons, a black businessman, led a successful term-limits initiative in Kansas City, Missouri, in 1990. Although the measure was attacked by black politicians as racist during the campaign, and upon winning was sued under the Voting Rights Act (the measure was upheld in federal court), after the term limits took effect the minority representation on the city council increased, as did the number of women serving.

The Michigan legislature is now under term limits that were passed only last year, but already lobbyists say that the legislature has changed. Commenting on the effect of term limits, Linda Gobbler, president of the Michigan Grocers Association, said:

> It becomes very important for lobbyists to be extremely credible, to have good reputations, and to know what they're talking about. Gone are the days when you belly up to the bar and ask somebody for a vote on a bill.[46]

Good riddance to those days.

Restoring Government 'Of the People'

When our nation began its experiment in government of, by, and for the people, no one could have known for certain the outcome. Thankfully, the freest, most prosperous nation in the history of human civilization was the result. Term limits, or mandatory rotation

---

[45]Jerry Gillam, "Term Limits Put Assembly 27 on Bipartisan Path," *Los Angeles Times,* March 15, 1993, pp. B1 and B4.

[46]Amy Baldwin, *Crain's Detroit Business,* November 1, 1993, p. 24.

in office, are part of a restoration of government of the people. No one can precisely predict the impact, but the preliminary indications show that the term limits will work—that is, they will restore a competitive election process and return Congress to a citizen legislature. Without term limits, Congress will surely not act to change its sizable election advantages. The idea of a citizen legislature, no matter how politicians and the political elite deride it, is alive and well with the American people who pay the bills and who are this country's rightful owners.

The American people care very deeply about the present state of our nation. In an effort to investigate the great deal of voter frustration regarding politics, the Kettering Foundation commissioned a study which found:

> Apathy is not rampant among citizens. A sense of civic duty is not dead. Americans are not indifferent to public debate and the challenges our nation faces. Americans simply want to participate in this process we call representative government.[47]

The American citizenry has carefully deliberated and debated the issue of term limits. At town meetings, on talk radio, on the editorial pages, and at the polls, the voters have spoken loud and clear. Yet, Congress has stonewalled at every turn because limits run counter to the members' personal career plans. In this crucial showdown between the people and the politicians, the people shall prevail.

"Congress as we know it," said the Brookings Institution's Thomas Mann, "is incompatible with a term-limited membership."[48] Yes, that's the point, and why I join 80 percent of the American people in supporting congressional term limits.

---

[47]Richard C. Harwood, "Citizens and Politics: A View from Main Street America," a study prepared for the Kettering Foundation by The Harwood Group, 1991 (emphasis in original). The study was conducted by holding 10 focus groups of 12 people in each representing a cross section demographically. The focus groups were held in Richmond, Va.; Philadelphia, Pa.; Des Moines, Iowa; Dallas, Tex.; Los Angeles, Calif.; Seattle, Wash.; Memphis, Tenn.; Denver, Colo.; Boston, Mass.; and Indianapolis, Ind.

[48]Hook.

4. Term Limits: Not the Answer to What Ails Politics

Becky Cain

Our political system is failing the American people. Citizens are disgusted—and they have every reason to be—with the role of special interests and "big money" in the political process, with the emptiness of modern political campaigns, and with our government's seeming inability to deal in a meaningful way with intractable national problems such as health care, crime, and a lackluster economy. And just as the American people have a number of very specific complaints about the ways in which government responds—or fails to respond—to their needs and concerns, so too are there a number of very specific things that we can do to fix the American political system. But alas, setting term limits for members of Congress is not one of them.

Term limits are a smokescreen, a simplistic answer to hard questions about our government, questions that demand equally hard choices. It is easy, as it always has been, to holler, "Throw the bums out!" It is a more thoughtful, complicated process, however, to throw out the pieces of the system that are corrupting or that don't work and to keep and strengthen what's good and productive about our government.

The truth is that we already have term limits in this country, and they are called elections. If we don't like the job that our elected representatives in Washington are doing, we can support other candidates and vote the incumbents out. While there is plenty that we can and must do to even the playing field between challengers and incumbents, we cannot ignore the fact that incumbents are regularly sent packing from Washington if they are perceived to have "lost touch" with the folks back home.

What's Wrong with Term Limits?

The term-limits movement's "meat-ax" approach does not distinguish between legislators whose careers deserve to be cut short and

45

those who deserve reelection. As a result, term limitations deny us the right to choose those who we think best represent us and our interests. The decision about how long in office is long enough should be left up to the voters, who are the best judges of whether their interests are being served by the women and men whom they send to Washington. Here's what else is wrong with term limits:

- Term limits would weaken the legislative branch of government—and strengthen an already powerful Presidency. Congress must be able to form its own judgments on national issues, to come to consensus independently of the executive branch's policies, if necessary. A Congress of amateurs, however, would by its very nature be more pliable and deferential—and the institution would thus be robbed of its historic role of restraining the power of the executive, who controls the entire federal bureaucracy. As a result, the branch of government closest to the people would become a less effective advocate for its constituents.

- Term limits would result in increased reliance on congressional staff and unelected "insiders." Novice legislators would depend much more on staff to sort out complicated issues and to keep things running—this at a time when many argue that congressional staffs are already too influential. Inexperienced representatives would also be forced to turn to Washington political insiders for advice on issues, meaning policy decisions and the oversight of complex financial markets and international affairs would in all probability end up largely in the hands of seasoned bureaucrats, presidential appointees, and judges. Also gaining in influence under term limits would be lobbyists and special interests.

- Term limits would inhibit meaningful congressional reforms. Instead of offering an opportunity to make productive changes in the political system, term limits would require legislators to exit the system just as they are developing a working knowledge of how it does and doesn't work—just as their developing understanding of the system would place them in a position to offer meaningful proposals for making it work better.

- Term limits ignore the need for enlightened and experienced management of public policy. There is nothing wrong with entrusting decisions about complex and crucial issues that can affect our lives and the world we live in to people with professional experience. We recognize the importance of experience in other walks of life—teachers are required to do student teaching, doctors have to complete residencies, and laborers have worked in apprenticeships for centuries. Why can't we expect the nation's lawmakers to benefit from experience when dealing with such complex matters as the world economy and meeting the needs of a modern society of 250 million diverse individuals?

- Term limits would put our elected officials in a position of always thinking about that "next job," giving them an excuse not to be responsive to the people who elect them. Elected representatives with a built-in cut-off date are less likely to be swayed by their constituents' interests and more likely to respond to the special interests who might provide them with a job—or at least, a hand in finding one—after their term is over. And for many, congressional service will become merely a stepping-stone to a higher office. From day one, term-limited legislators would make decisions—and would be forced to make decisions—not necessarily with their constituents' interests in mind but with an eye to their own interests for the future. Instead of having "career politicians" who are committed to the institutions in which they serve, we would have career politicians with an overriding commitment to their careers.

- Term limits would limit the field of potential candidates for public office. Running for and holding public office is too expensive, too life-disrupting, too privacy-invading, and too time-consuming to become a popular "sabbatical" choice for dedicated and serious professionals in other fields. Therefore, the only candidates attracted to run for term-limited offices would be the rich or the retired. Take a look at the top political appointments in the executive branch. Despite the fact that those term-limited positions offer prestigious opportunities for government service without the price of running for office, we still have had no surplus of high-quality people seeking and/or accepting the jobs. Rather, qualified appointees who are eager to accept those positions are becoming harder and harder to find, let alone to keep.

- Term limits would encourage legislators to consider the short term over the long term. Finally, term-limited legislators would know for certain that they wouldn't be around to deal with the long-term consequences of many of their decisions. Their limited time in office would encourage them to focus on "quick fixes" and programs that might be wildly popular at the moment but that might result in severe repercussions down the road.

If Not Term Limits, Then What?

Political reality—or at least many of the grim realities that have infected our political system in recent years—is certainly worth questioning, challenging, and working to change. It is just that term limitations are not what we need. They might, in fact, add to what's wrong with the way things now stand.

Rather, comprehensive campaign finance reform is a real solution to many of the problems that the backers of term limits are seeking to address. Unlike term limits, campaign finance reform is a solution that will yield important and immediate improvements in how politics is conducted in this country. The closer you look at many of the problems people point to when arguing for term limits, the clearer it becomes that campaign finance reform is the better answer. Campaign finance reform, for example, has the potential of substantially diminishing the power of incumbency—a key objective of supporters of term limits—by placing limits on the amount of money an incumbent may spend, by making public funds and other resources such as free air time available to challengers, and by putting caps on the special-interest contributions that are disproportionately directed to those who are already in power.

Americans are disheartened by the fact that national campaigns have become more expensive—and more exclusive—with the passing of every election season. In the 1992 congressional races, campaign spending by U.S. Senate and House candidates during the fall general-election contests topped $500 million, $113 million more than was spent during the entire 1990 election cycle.

The effects of skyrocketing campaign costs are clear and disturbing. Qualified challengers are deterred from running, and competition suffers. In particular, women and minorities, often the challengers, are frequently prevented from running competitive races because of insufficient funds. The "money chase" also means that candidates are lured more and more toward special-interest contributions and all of the strings attached to them. And finally, legislators who are

48

forced always to be thinking about fundraising for the next election inevitably spend less and less time communicating with and serving their constituents.

If we are truly going to increase government accountability to citizens and restore faith in a discredited system, the day-to-day influence of special interests on our legislators must be curbed. It is time once and for all for Congress to put the American people before big-money contributors by passing fundamental campaign finance reform legislation. There can be no excuse for allowing the current campaign finance mess to continue. Spending limits are needed to restrain escalating campaign costs and to allow challengers to compete. And candidates must receive public financing for their campaigns so that they can get their messages to voters without having to depend on special-interest money.

Public financing of congressional elections will return citizens and voters to their central role in the political process. It will tell candidates that they do not have to go to the highest bidder to raise the funds they need to compete. Awarded with no strings attached, public financing is the cleanest money in American politics, the only effective way to reduce special-interest influence while making sure that candidates are able to offer voters the information they need to make an informed decision on election day.

Another effective way to reform campaign financing while reining in the influence of special interests in elections and government in this country is by limiting political action committee (PAC) contributions. The percentage of congressional candidates' receipts coming from PACs has been steadily increasing in recent elections, meaning that after the elections, our elected leaders are increasingly beholden to the vested interests who bankrolled their campaigns. Losing influence and interest as the PAC spending has accelerated have been we citizens who actually put the representatives in office with our votes.

Unlike term limits, campaign finance reform is a solution that will yield important and immediate improvements in how politics is conducted in this country. The closer you look at many of the problems people point to when arguing for term limits, the clearer it becomes that campaign finance reform is the better answer. Campaign finance reform, for example, has the potential for substantially diminishing the power of incumbency—a key objective of supporters of term limits—by placing limits on the amount of money an incumbent may spend, by making public funds and other resources such as free air time available to challengers, and by putting caps on the special-interest contributions that are disproportionately directed to those who are already in power.

Only by enacting comprehensive campaign reform can Congress reduce the influence of special interests in the legislative process, ensure fair political competition, and welcome the public back into the political process.

Overcoming Voter Disillusionment

The job of improving American politics will not be completed, however, when campaign finance reforms are enacted. In addition to reforming the way we pay for political campaigns in this country, we need to reform and rethink the way we run them—and the way they are presented to the American public. We need to pry campaign rhetoric away from the seven-second sound bite and instead anchor our political discourse in substance. We need less mudslinging and more platform building in campaigns so that we elect representatives with clear mandates from the people and with promises to keep and missions to carry out on our behalf.

Although voter turnout in the 1992 election was the highest recorded in 20 years, just over half of Americans who were eligible to vote went to the polls. Furthermore, nearly 70 million Americans are still not even registered to vote. Even after all the euphoria and optimism about citizen participation and involvement that surrounded the 1992 election, it's clear that too many Americans continue to think that their votes don't matter. They are disillusioned by their government's apparent inability to act, disgusted by all the negative campaigning and name-calling, and disturbed by the difficulty they have in obtaining useful information—the information they need to make informed choices in the voting booth and to participate in a substantive way in the nation's public-policy debates.

In short, Americans are not indifferent, apathetic, or "lazy." Rather, as we saw again in November 1993, they are angry and rebellious—rebellious because they have been edged out of the democratic process. The lines of communication and accountability between citizens and government have broken down. Citizens aren't talking because government isn't listening.

That was the key finding of a June 1993 poll conducted by the League of Women Voters in cooperation with Post-It™ Brand Tape

Flags, a division of the 3M Company. Entitled "Action or Apathy," the poll was crafted to measure citizens' attitudes about government and about their perceived impact on politics. Alarmingly, over 80 percent of respondents said they felt they had little influence in setting national public policy; most were of the opinion that lobbyists and public-interest groups run the show.

Similarly, in a new report from the Kettering Foundation called "College Students Talk Politics," many of the nation's young Americans told researchers that they have little real interest in participating in the political process. Among their complaints: "It's not productive to participate" . . . "Campaigns are for name-calling and backbiting" . . . "What you hear from public officials has little connection to what they'll do once in office" . . . "Organized interests have locked up the political process." The list goes on and on. The only way to be heard, the students agreed, was through protest.

The Importance of Debates

So what ever happened to the idea of the political campaign as a forum for discussion of important issues? Although it is sometimes easy to forget in this era of calculated and often crass political appeals, campaigns *should* be about educating voters—both about the issues at stake and about the candidates' plans and positions and the experience they would bring to their jobs.

For campaigns to be educational and to nurture real dialogue between voters and candidates, we need to create opportunities for both sides to talk and listen. Candidate debates are the best such opportunities we have. A debate that functions as a presentation and a testing ground for ideas—and not as a rehearsed campaign commercial—can be of more use to both voters and candidates than virtually any other aspect of the modern political campaign. For the voters, a debate can showcase the experience and the thinking of candidates and contrast their varying opinions, platforms, and styles of dealing with tough issues. And, time and again, candidates have observed that preparing for a debate—digging deeply into the issues of the campaign, thinking through their positions and the reasoning behind them—focuses them on what's important in the election and, incidentally, removes them from the fundraising trail and the "ad battles" to engage in real substance.

Our elected officials cannot govern effectively by sound bite. A seven-second response might work fine on the evening news but it doesn't hold up in the face of economic hardship, health care concerns, international crises, homelessness, increases in violent crime—or even a proliferation of potholes on city streets. We need elected officials who can handle the complex business of governing and who can articulate the problems and alternative solutions clearly. And clearly, the campaign debate is the best forum we have for assessing the abilities of our representatives-to-be in these critical areas. And while the League of Women Voters is wary of legislative or other proposals compelling candidates to debate, we do feel it is a candidate's duty to face his opponents—and that she or he should suffer the consequences—from opponents, from the public, and from the news media—of not debating.

The full burden for open dialogue and meaningful campaigning does not rest with the candidates alone, however. The news media, for one, have a very real responsibility to report on the substance of political campaigns—to present voters with the information they need to make informed choices. It is easy to cast political coverage in the vernacular of the horse race, but it is also irresponsible. Time and again, we have seen how reliance on polling data and a "who's up, who's down" approach to political reporting diminishes the process and diverts attention away from the issues. To their credit, American journalists were among the first to note the dangers of this kind of coverage, and many are trying to turn things around.

Voters need more in-depth reporting about candidates' ideas and close scrutiny of their speeches and, if they are incumbents, their records in office. We need substantive evaluations of social conditions, economic progress, education, and fiscal responsibility—all the complicated, unsexy, necessary business that goes into governing and meeting constituents' needs and concerns. And we need reliable critiques of paid advertising and of the candidates' claims and counterclaims. Providing these things should be the overriding duty of campaign journalists and their news organizations. And the coverage shouldn't stop once the election is over. The media should hold candidates and officeholders accountable because that would work better than term limits or anything else in showing voters whether somebody truly deserves reelection.

The Real Campaign Trail: What Citizens Can Do

By redirecting media attention from the polls and the sound bites and the diversionary battles over things that don't really matter, we can get moving on the real campaign trail—the one where candidates engage the voters in a meaningful dialogue (and where both learn from it), the one where voters turn out to make their choices at the polls, and the one that we can follow to better, more representative, and more responsive government.

Citizens, of course, are not without their own role in making the trip down the real campaign trail a fruitful one for all involved. Citizens have to recognize their role in their own empowerment— by keeping abreast of pressing national issues that can affect their future, by keeping track of important policy proposals and making their opinions on them known, and by making every effort to learn more about their elected officials and the women and men who might challenge them. Citizen action can have a profound effect on the strength and effectiveness of our democracy, but if we are not educated about the issues, about the candidates, and about the ways in which we can make a difference, then things are not likely to change.

If people feel a connection between themselves and their government, they will participate. And they will vote. Nonpartisan, political education is thus a critical precursor to widespread citizen activism and an antidote to the concerns that have given rise to people's passion for term limits. We continually need to remind all citizens that the power of change is in their hands. And we must start when they are young, before the seeds of alienation are planted.

From a very early age, children in this country are taught about government and politics not by witnessing participation in action, but from the civics texts that have been an American classroom staple for much of this century. Rather than learning what voting and activism mean and why they're worthwhile, kids are instead being asked to memorize the meanings of words such as "filibuster" and "pork barrel." And rather than understanding citizen participation as a vital and exciting aspect of democracy—an opportunity to make a difference—they come to see it as some new boring duty they are supposed to bear, like flossing their teeth or cleaning their rooms.

Young people don't need to hear another lecture about the burden of responsibility. They need to hear how rewarding and fun citizen activism can be. Politics and government should be taught as an exciting, interactive activity. Children need firsthand experience creating positive change in their neighborhoods and communities; they need to get involved.

The League of Women Voters of Minnesota has challenged conventional wisdom with a newly developed social studies curriculum entitled "We've Got the Power: Skills for Democracy." Not your run-of-the-mill social studies class, this creative program actually gives students firsthand experience in consensus building, negotiation, respect for minorities, and individual responsibility. The idea is to teach not just civics but the rewards of citizenship.

These are lessons, frankly, that all Americans could put to use. By educating citizens young and old about the issues and about the many ways in which citizens can make a difference, we can go a long way to building a more informed electorate and a more responsive government without patronizing people with term-limit schemes that take away their true right to choose.

Eliminating Barriers to Participation

But what good is a program to encourage citizens to get involved in government if many of them are still discouraged from voting? Too many Americans who want to vote cannot because of stubborn barriers to registration such as these:

- In Boulder, Colorado, only handicapped voters can register by mail, requiring the rest of the population to find the time in their workdays to register in person.
- In Stamford, Connecticut, election officials turned down a League of Women Voters request to set up a registration site at a shelter for the homeless.
- And in many other areas, Leagues report that registration officials have adopted "an attitude" about their jobs and function. They are discouraging, unwelcoming, and not helpful, Leagues say, when it comes to making it easy and convenient—and even possible—for citizens to register.

It is no wonder that increasing numbers of Americans "have an attitude" about registering and voting. These bureaucratic barriers must come down. And thanks to the determined efforts of thousands of members of the League of Women Voters from across the country and to other grassroots organizations such as the NAACP, not to mention the leadership and support of key members of Congress, many of these barriers will come down with the implementation of the National Voter Registration Act. Thanks to this new law, which will take effect in 1995, millions of eligible Americans will be able to apply to register to vote for federal elections when applying for or renewing a driver's license or nondriver ID, by mail, and at selected government agencies.

With between 85 and 87 percent of all registered voters voting in recent presidential elections, the National Voter Registration Act is sure to have a positive effect on voter turnout and citizen participation. And that's a good thing, because the United States has one of the lowest levels of voter participation among industrialized democracies.

No "Quick Fixes"

The National Voter Registration Act was founded on the belief that citizens need to participate in government in this country. The more that citizens participate, the more government is responsive to their concerns and the less we need to hear about term limits and other "quick-fix" solutions to what ails politics.

American citizens are tired of being force-fed simplistic political rhetoric. They want to hear the whole story, the straight story. They want the facts—all the facts—so they can understand the difficult choices that need to be made as we look ahead to this nation's future. And they want to know that their elected officials are beholden only to them, and not to powerful moneyed interests. An electorate that is assured of these things—and that is freely able to make its opinions known—can make its own decisions about when and whether to end a representative's term in office.

If the American people are impatient, it is because they have been led on by slick sound bites that promise change overnight and by politicians who don't tell the truth or who shade their true positions and beliefs for fear they might lose an election. The distortions and the impossible promises, however, have made us all losers. And they must come to an end.

It is time for some honest, up-front communication between citizens and government. And it is time for real accountability and results. By fixing what's wrong with the system and by keeping what works (including those politicians who are doing a good job and deserve to be reelected), the voters get the best of all possible

worlds. And that's what campaigns and elections—and governing—
are all about.

Term limits are a limited notion that limits our choices as voters.
We need more choices, not fewer. And we don't need to give up
on the system—we need to take it back.

5. Restoring "The University in Rotation": An Essay in Defense of Term Limitation

Mark P. Petracca

Term limitation is undoubtedly the twentieth century's most popular institutional reform as evidenced by both election results and opinion polls. Since 1990, fifteen states have passed initiatives limiting terms for federal legislators, including California, Michigan, Florida, Ohio, and Washington. Sixteen states have also adopted term limits for state legislators in the last four years, most recently in Maine.[1] Moreover, voters in a growing number of municipalities have brought term limits to City Hall. At least 35 percent of the 60 largest U.S. cities, including New York, Los Angeles, Houston, New Orleans, and San Francisco, now have term limits for local elected officials.

Opinion polls tell a similar story. Various opinion polls conducted during the last four years show that anywhere from 70 to 80 percent of the American public support term limits and this strong level of support is uniform regardless of political party, race, ethnicity, income, gender, or geographical location. When it comes specifically to Congress, a *Wall Street Journal*/NBC poll in April of 1992 showed that 80 percent of Americans favor a limit on congressional terms.

I want to thank Jenny Dixon, Julie Chaicharee, Rod Attebery, and Chad Kunimoto for their research assistance.

[1]Fourteen states limit terms for *both* state and federal legislators: Arizona, Arkansas, California, Colorado, Florida, Michigan, Missouri, Montana, Nebraska, Ohio, Oregon, South Dakota, Washington, and Wyoming. North Dakota has term limits only for its federal legislators; Oklahoma and Maine only for state legislators. For an overview of the term-limits movement, see Mark P. Petracca and Darci Jump, "Term Limitation Express," *Society* 31 (November/December 1993): 61–69; and James Coyne and John H. Fund, *Cleaning House: America's Campaign for Term Limits* (Washington, D.C.: Regnery Gateway, 1992).

In May of 1993 the firm of Fabrizio, McLaughlin & Associates found a 76 percent approval rating for congressional term limits.[2]

Not since states acted unilaterally to begin directly electing their U.S. senators at the beginning of this century, a movement culminating in adoption of the Seventeenth Amendment to the U.S. Constitution in 1913, has there been such a burst of grassroots activity from coast to coast directed at institutional and constitutional reform. Much to the dismay of entrenched incumbents and confounded critics, the term-limits movement has become a durable and potent part of the American political landscape.

Of course, the electorate and the general public could be wrong about the wisdom and prudence of term limitation. As term-limits critics are quick to point out, "Americans in large majorities also like the idea of . . . abolishing the electoral college, banning flag burning, [and] repealing the Bill of Rights." Hence, "Few would argue that the support of the American people for an idea is itself a sufficient condition to pass a law or change the Constitution."[3] Fair enough. After all, political scientists have repeatedly documented (and in excruciating detail) the widespread ignorance of the American public when it comes to matters of politics and public policy. Unfortunately, this view predisposes many political scientists to be suspicious of any reform idea supported by the public, particularly term limitation.[4]

If term limitation were a bad idea, neither election victories nor a high level of public support would make it any better. However, *this time* the public may be right, notwithstanding the hyperbolized warnings of term-limits critics. Term limitation should be endorsed as a way to reestablish one of the most fundamental principles of

[2]For an interesting public-choice explanation for the popularity of term limits, see A. Dick and J. Lott, "Reconciling Voters' Behavior and Legislative Term Limits," *Journal of Public Economics* 50 (January 1993): 1–14. Dick and Lott explain why voters simultaneously vote for term limits and reelect their own incumbent. Support for term limits is also examined in Malcolm Jewell, "Sources of Support for Term Limitations in State Legislatures," Paper presented at the Annual Meeting of the Southwestern Political Science Association, New Orleans, La., March 17–20, 1993.

[3]Testimony by Norman J. Ornstein before the House Judiciary Subcommittee on Civil and Constitutional Rights, November 18, 1993, p. 1.

[4]See Mark P. Petracca, "Predisposed to Oppose: Political Scientists and Term Limitations," *Polity* 24 (Summer 1992): 657–72. For a strong antidote to this view, see Benjamin I. Page and Robert Y. Shapiro, *The Rational Public* (Chicago: University of Chicago Press, 1992).

republican political design—rotation in office—and as an appropriate antidote to the professionalization of political representation in American legislatures.

Rotation in the American Political Tradition

The principle of rotation in office, historical antecedent of modern term limitation, is based upon the simple, but profound Aristotelian observation that democratic citizenship is possible only where there is a reciprocity "of ruling and being ruled by turn." It is a principle deeply rooted in the development of democratic political institutions and is squarely within the American political tradition.[5]

Promoted by Aristotle and Cicero as a fundamental characteristic of democratic government, practiced in ancient Athens and Rome along with the Renaissance city-states of Florence and Venice, rotation in office was widely praised as an essential component of classical republican political design by a wide array of distinguished English writers during the seventeenth and eighteenth centuries, including James Harrington, John Milton, John Locke, William Blackstone, William Godwin, Walter Moyle, Algernon Sidney, Henry Neville, James Burgh, and John Trenchard among others.

American Precedents. In the "new world" of the seventeenth and eighteenth centuries, limits on the terms of officeholders or required rotation in office were viewed as a characteristic of legislative and deliberative institutions in many colonial, revolutionary, and post-revolutionary charters, treaties, and constitutions.

Practiced by the Dutch in New Amsterdam and during the colonial period in New York, rotation was found in the *New England Confederation of 1643*, in William Penn's "Frame of Government" (1682; article III) for Pennsylvania, and the Delaware "Frame of Government" (1683). Upon returning from the First Continental Congress in 1774, John Adams recommended that future conventions follow the principle of rotation: "I am for making of it annual, and for Sending an entire new set every Year, that all the principal Genius's may go to the University in Rotation—that We may have Politicians in Plenty."[6]

---

[5]All citations in this section, except where otherwise noted, may be found in Mark P. Petracca, "Rotation in Office: The History of an Idea," in *Limiting Legislative Terms*, ed. Gerald Benjamin and Michael J. Malbin (Washington, D.C.: CQ Press, 1992), pp. 19–51.

[6]John Adams, "To James Warren, June 25, 1774," in *Papers of John Adams*, vol. 2, ed. Robert J. Taylor (Cambridge, Mass.: Harvard University Press, 1977), p. 100.

Support for rotation grew in revolutionary America. The Pennsylvania Constitution of 1776, authored by Benjamin Franklin, required rotation in office for state officeholders, including legislators, in order to avoid "the danger of establishing an inconvenient aristocracy." Similarly, the Maryland Declaration of Rights of 1776 (article XXXI) imposed a mandatory rotation on executive departments, stating: "That a long continuance in the first executive departments of power or trust, is dangerous to liberty; a rotation, therefore, in those departments, is one of the best securities of permanent freedom." Indeed, the expectation or requirement that elected officials would soon "return" to "private life" or "private station" was contained in the bills of rights accompanying six of the new state constitutions adopted from 1776 to 1780. The Virginia Bill of Rights, for example, provided that members of the legislature and executive "may be restrained from oppression, by feeling and participating the burdens of the people, they should, at fixed periods, be reduced to private station" (1776, section 5). Similar provisions appeared in the bills of rights accompanying the constitutions of Pennsylvania (1776, articles 19 and 11); Delaware (1776, article 4); New York (1777, article 11); South Carolina (1778, article 9); and Massachusetts (1780, article 8).

Influenced by the writings of Harrington and Burgh, along with views widely held in Massachusetts, John Adams endorsed frequent elections and rotation in office as the principal means of keeping government as near to the people as possible. With typical eloquence, Adams captured the importance of both principles on the eve of the American Revolution in 1776:

> Elections, especially of representatives and counsellors, should be annual, there not being in the whole circle of the sciences a maxim more infallible than this, 'where annual elections end, there slavery begins.' These great men ... should be one a year—Like bubbles on the sea of matter borne, They rise, they break, and to that sea return. This will teach them the great political virtues of humility, patience, and moderation, without which every man in power becomes a ravenous beast of prey.

This constellation of republican sentiments influenced the drafting of the Articles of Confederation (1781) which called for the annual appointment of delegates, provided for their recall at any time, and set limits on the length of time a delegate could hold office. Article

Five of the Articles stated: "No state shall be represented in Congress by less than two, nor more than seven members; and no person shall be capable of being a delegate for more than three years in any term of six years." Thomas Jefferson, among others, praised the principle of rotation contained in the Articles which was also "established in the office of President of Congress, who could serve but one in three."

The Advantages of Rotation. Throughout the historical development of democratic theory and the design of republican governments, three main advantages have been attributed to the principle of rotation in office: (1) it checks the abuse of public power by frequently returning officeholders to private station; (2) it increases the opportunity for citizens to serve in public office, thereby expanding the educative function of political participation; and (3) it enhances the overall quality of political representation by creating a reciprocity of responsibility and experience among rulers and the ruled. These advantages were well understood and greatly appreciated by a diverse group of American revolutionaries and constitutional Framers, most prominently, Thomas Paine, John Adams, Thomas Jefferson, Benjamin Franklin, Elbridge Gerry, George Mason, Melancton Smith, James Madison, and George Washington.[7]

"The truth is," said a Committee of Congress in 1782, "the security intended to the general liberty in the Confederation consists in the frequent election and in the rotation of the members of Congress, by which there is a constant and effective check upon them. This is the security which the people in every state enjoy against the usurpations of their internal government and it is the true source of security in a representative republic."[8] Three members of Congress authored this declaration in support of rotation, Thomas Fitzsimmons of Pennsylvania, James Madison of Virginia, and Alexander Hamilton of New York.

[7]Support for the principle of rotation continued following final ratification of the Constitution in 1791. Presidents Washington, Jefferson, Monroe, Jackson, Polk, Buchanan, and Lincoln all praised and variously practiced the rotative principle along with other prominent Americans, such as John Taylor, William Crawford, and Frederick Grimke. Moreover, support for rotation was not limited to America. English writers Edmund Burke, John Stuart Mill, and James Bryce were also favorably disposed to rotation. Rotation was also a key feature in the French Constitutions of 1791 and 1795 following the Revolution.

[8]Quoted in Charles Warren, *The Making of the Constitution* (Cambridge, Mass.: Harvard University Press, 1937), p. 363.

Thus, contrary to the persistent assertion of term-limits critics, there is absolutely nothing un-American about term limitation, based as it is upon the "truly republican principle of rotation in office."

Explaining the Absence of Rotation in the Constitution. This discussion still leaves us with a perplexing question. If rotation was such a popular and widely accepted political principle, why then was it omitted as a requirement from the U.S. Constitution? After all, a requirement for rotation was contained in the Virginia Plan submitted by Edmund Randolph.[9] Moreover, when Rufus King, Nathaniel Gorham, and Elbridge Gerry, the delegates from Massachusetts to the Constitutional Convention, left for Philadelphia in the spring of 1787, they were under strict instruction from the Massachusetts legislature "not to depart from the rotation established" in the Articles of Confederation.[10] What happened to the provision in Randolph's plan and the instruction given to the delegates from Massachusetts?

After rather brief debate on different occasions throughout the summer of 1787, neither mandatory rotation nor ineligibility for office was included in subsequent drafts of the Constitution for either the House or the executive, nor explicitly for the Senate. Thomas Jefferson pointed out this weakness in the proposed Constitution to James Madison in a letter dated December 20, 1787: "The second feature I dislike, and greatly dislike, is the abandonment in every instance of the necessity of rotation in office, and most particularly in the case of the President."

In deciding not to include a requirement for rotation in the new Constitution, Convention delegates did not reject the principle or importance of rotation in office. In fact, the record indicates that only a small number of delegates to the Constitutional Convention and subsequent state ratification conventions expressed opposition to the rotative principle, most prominently Alexander Hamilton.

How can we account for the absence of a requirement for mandatory rotation in the Constitution?

First, the requirement of rotation had been difficult to enforce during the fragile period of national union under the Articles of Confederation. The Framers of the Constitution were rightly wary

---

[9]A requirement for rotation also appeared in plans for a new government submitted by Charles Pinckney of South Carolina and William Patterson of New Jersey.

[10]Warren, *The Making of the Constitution,* p. 613.

of imposing any further requirements on the states which, if difficult to enforce, could threaten the stability and governability of the new union.

Second, as John Fund has explained, requirements for mandatory rotation were left out of the Constitution "largely because they were thought of as 'entering too much into detail' for a short document."[11] ✗

Third, delegates to the Convention thought mandatory rotation unnecessary given short terms, the doctrine of instruction,[12] and the other checks built into the Constitution, such as the separation of powers and federalism.[13]

Fourth, with specific reference to the Senate, the Framers may have expected article I, section 3 of the Constitution to provide for a full rotation of that body every six years, exactly as proposed by James Harrington in *Oceana* (1656). James Wilson of Pennsylvania responded to delegates opposed to the long terms being proposed for Senators with this explanation: "There is a rotation; and every second year one third of the whole number go out. Every fourth year two thirds of them are changed. In six years, the whole body is supplied a new one."[14] This explanation turned into an expectation for Fisher Ames when he recommended adoption of the proposed Constitution to the Massachusetts ratification convention in January of 1788:

> A very effectual check upon the power of the Senate is pro-
> vided. A third part is *to retire* from office every two years.
> By this means, while senators are seated for six years, they are

[11]John Fund, "Term Limitation: An Idea Whose Time Has Come," *Cato Institute Policy Analysis* 141 (October 30, 1990): 1.

[12]The prevalent doctrine of instruction entailed the right of electors to impose binding instructions on their representatives. The theory and practice of instruction is discussed at length in John Phillip Reid, *The Concept of Representation in the Age of the American Revolution* (Chicago: University of Chicago Press, 1989).

[13]A similar argument was used by Hamilton to explain why the proposed Constitution did not contain a bill of rights. See Mark P. Petracca, "What Americans Should Know About the Bill of Rights: Eight Lessons," *this Constitution* (Fall 1991): 54–58.

[14]Jonathan Elliot, *The Debates in the Several State Conventions on the Adoption of the Federal Constitution*, vol. 2 (New York: Burt Franklin, 1968 from the original 1888 publication), p. 477. Other delegates, such as George Read, James McHenry, and Edmund Randolph, also interpreted this section of the Constitution to imply a triennial rotation of the Senate. See Max Farrand, ed., *The Records of the Federal Convention of 1787* (1911; New Haven, Conn.: Yale University Press; 1966), vol. 1, p. 421; vol. 3, p. 147; and vol. 1, p. 408.

admonished of their responsibility to the state legislatures. If one third new members are introduced, who will feel the sentiments of their states, they will awe that third whose term will be near expiring (emphasis added).[15]

This clause of the Constitution was also interpreted by legal scholars and historians throughout the nineteenth century as creating a full rotation in the Senate every six years. "The next clause" in article I, section 3 "of the Constitution," explained Joseph Story, "provides for a change of one third of the members every two years. Thus the whole body is gradually changed in the course of six years, always retaining a larger portion of experience, and yet incapable of combining its members together for sinister purposes."[16] The Constitution permits reelection of senators; however, there was a clear expectation, by constitutional Framers and subsequent commentators, that a full rotation of the Senate would occur every six years.

Finally, and most importantly, the prevalent practice of voluntary rotation in many states and during the Confederation may have persuaded most delegates that rotation in office would be the norm in the new national government, with or without a constitutional requirement. This expectation is expressed clearly in President George Washington's First Inaugural Address. Praising various provisions of the new Constitution which would lessen "the opportunity for corruption and influence," Washington assured: "Nor can the members of Congress exempt themselves from consequences of any unjust and tyrannical acts which they may impose upon others. For in a short time they will mingle with the mass of the people. Their interests must therefore be the same, and their feelings in sympathy with those of their Constituents."[17]

Throughout most of the nineteenth century, voluntary rotation in office was the prevailing norm and standard of behavior for national legislators—even by those luminaries of the U.S. Congress whose

[15]Seth Ames, *Works of Fisher Ames*, vol. 1, ed. W.B. Allen (Indianapolis, Ind.: Liberty Fund, 1983), p. 548.

[16]Joseph Story, *A Familiar Exposition of the Constitution of the United States* (New York: Harper & Bros, 1893, originally published in 1840), p. 72. Further substantiation for this expectation can be found in George Bancroft, *History of the United States of America*, vol. 6 (New York: D. Appleton and Co., 1885), p. 245; and Charles K. Burdick, *The Law of the American Constitution* (New York: G.P. Putnam's Sons, 1922), p. 163.

[17]W.B. Allen, ed., *George Washington: A Collection* (Indianapolis, Ind.: Liberty Fund, 1988), p. 448.

cumulative service in elected office was quite lengthy, such as John Calhoun, Daniel Webster, and Henry Clay.[18] National officeholders did not make careers out of service in either the House or Senate, preferring instead to serve for brief periods, from one to two terms, and then voluntarily retire to take different elected positions or pursue other endeavors. Indeed, through the end of the nineteenth century it was rare for the percentage of first-term members to be lower than 40 to 45 percent.

A Response to the Hamiltonian Critique. Against this backdrop of support for the principle and practice of rotation in office stands Alexander Hamilton's opposition to rotation. "Rotation," said Hamilton, "would be a diminution of the inducements to good behavior." It would tempt "sordid views" and "peculation," by officeholders who think about nothing else but where their next job will be. Finally, Hamilton echoed concerns heard repeatedly in the debate over term limits: rotation would deprive the nation of "the experience and wisdom gained by an incumbent, perhaps just when that experience is needed most."

Though primarily a defense of reeligibility for the executive, Hamilton's writings, along with remarks by New York's Robert R. Livingston and Connecticut's Roger Sherman, constitute the main historical evidence opponents of term limits have to explain the absence of rotation in the Constitution and to criticize the rotative principle. This is understandable because Hamilton was one of the only American revolutionaries or constitutional Framers opposed to rotation, at least for whom we have any written records. Frankly, this dependence upon Hamilton's political views is peculiar for a number of reasons.

First, having previously endorsed rotation as "the true source of security in a representative republic" we might be a little suspicious of Hamilton's reversal of judgment. Perhaps Hamilton was authentically opposed to rotation. Or, perhaps, as he did so often and well with other parts of the Constitution, he was simply defending its absence against strong criticism by the Antifederalists.[19]

---

[18]There were certainly exceptions to the rule. In the House, John Quincy Adams served 16 years after serving as President. In the Senate, Thomas Hart Benton served 30 years and Charles Sumner 24 years. But these are notable precisely because they were exceptions to the prevailing norm of voluntary rotation.

[19]Adding further confusion to Hamilton's view is a provision for rotation which appears in one copy of his plan for a new government. See Farrand, *The Records*, vol. 1, p. 309.

Second, Hamilton was certainly no friend of republican government and said so himself at the Convention during a discussion of term lengths for members of the Senate: "I acknowledge I do not think favorably of republican government; but I address my remarks to those who do, in order to prevail on them to tone their government as high as possible."[20] Yet, over Hamilton's objections, the convention delegates created a republican form of government in the Constitution and guaranteed the same to "every State in this Union" (article IV, section 4).

Third, Hamilton's views on a number of key features of institutional design were out of step with prevalent political attitudes. It's no great surprise he opposed rotation. His plan for a new national government called for both the President and members of the Senate to serve "during good behavior," without any specified term of office. In other words, Hamilton wanted Presidents and senators to serve for life! Moreover, he proposed the "Governor or president of each State" to be appointed by the newly established federal government. Indeed, few of the ideas for institutional design presented by Hamilton at the convention became part of the Constitution presented to the states for ratification.

Antifederalist writings and speeches also provided direct responses to the three arguments made by Hamilton, Livingston, and Sherman in opposition to rotation: (1) the people have a right to judge whom they will and will not elect to public office; (2) rotation reduces the incentives for political accountability; and (3) rotation deprives the polity of experienced public servants.

There were two prevalent responses to the first argument. First, states imposed many other restrictions on who could be elected to office so the requirement for rotation would hardly constitute a unique imposition.[21] Second, citizens could not always be relied upon to bring about the turnover in elected officials necessary to fulfill the other values of rotation. Richard Henry Lee explained:

> Were the people always properly attentive, they would at proper periods, call their law makers home, by sending others in their room; but it is not often the case, and therefore,

[20]Bancroft, *History of the United States of America*, vol. 6, p. 246.

[21]A contemporary evaluation of this criticism can be found in Mark P. Petracca, "Do Term Limits 'Rob Voters of Democratic Rights?' An Evaluation and Response," *Western State University Law Review* 20 (1993): 547–67.

> in making constitutions, when the people are attentive, they
> ought cautiously to provide for these benefits, those advanta-
> geous changes in the administration of their affairs, which
> they are often apt to be inattentive to in practice.

Lee, like many other Antifederalists, understood that incumbency
or "place" could be a powerful deterrent to meaningful electoral
competition and legislative turnover.

Melancton Smith and Richard Henry Lee also found the accountability critique easy to rebut. First, even if some incentive for accountability were lost, it would be worth the price to safeguard liberty.
Second, since elected officials would have to return home after stepping down from elected office, it's unlikely they would be inclined
to do anything in office against the interests of their constituents.
In fact, just the opposite would be true, making "a return to private
station" an inducement to good behavior and accountability rather
than a distraction from it.

Finally, the argument about the loss of experience and expertise
appeared to be the most specious given an accurate understanding of
the rotative principle. In a system of rotation, a person serves for a
specified period and is then forced to take a break, or as Jefferson put
it, "go out" of office. Rotation systems did not necessarily require
permanent retirement from public life, nor even from a specific office.
Rather than squandering experience, the capacity of the individual as
a representative and citizen—in keeping with the Aristotelian defense
of rotation—was enhanced by a periodic return to private station.

The Hamiltonian argument about the loss of experienced legislators presupposed that only a limited number of individuals were
presumptively qualified to service in office. To which Lee responded:
"I would not urge the principle of rotation, if I believed the consequence would be an uninformed federal legislature; but I have no
apprehension of this in this enlightened country." Contemporary
legislators may think they are the best, if not the only, persons
capable of representing the constituents from their district or state.
This is precisely the sort of hubris Antifederalists predicted would
develop among the elected aristocracy absent provisions for mandatory periodic rotation.

The Problem: Permanent Government

American legislatures have changed. The institutionalization of
the House and Senate began in the late nineteenth century and the

widespread professionalization of state legislatures began in the late 1950s.[22] Term-limits advocates begin their case for reform and a return to the principle of rotation in office by pointing to reelection rates for members of the House of Representatives (96.1 percent in 1990), the percentage of House members who return to office each legislative term (89.9 percent in 1990), and the declining rates of turnover and electoral competition in state legislatures.

The argument on behalf of term limits is simple. When a legislative body has a near-perfect reelection rate and no significant turnover, elections lose their meaning as a device to assure political accountability, discouraging citizen participation as a further consequence.

Representative democracy requires electoral competition and the dependence of legislators on the people. But electoral competition is no longer possible in a system where the benefits and power of incumbency virtually guarantee a lifelong career as a legislator. The problem is not individual incumbents, but rather, chronic incumbency.[23] Incumbents have extraordinary advantages in securing reelection over their opposition, if any. They are advantaged, explained Thomas Mann of the Brookings Institution, not only by a marked "decline in partisanship among voters," but also, by successfully "utilizing the increased resources at their disposal (staff, the franking

---

[22]See Nelson W. Polsby, "The Institutionalization of the U.S. House of Representatives," *American Political Science Review* 62 (March 1968): 144–68; Allan G. Bogue, Jerome M. Clubb, Carroll R. McKibbin, and Santa A. Traugott, "Members of the House of Representatives and the Processes of Modernization, 1789–1960," *Journal of American History* 63 (1976): 275–302; Richard G. Niemi and Laura R. Winsky, "Membership Turnover in U.S. State Legislatures: Trends and Effects of Districting," *Legislative Studies Quarterly* 12 (February 1987): 115–23; and Alan Rosenthal, "The Legislative Institution: Transformed and at Risk," in *The State of the States*, ed. Carl E. Van Horn (Washington, D.C.: CQ Press, 1989), pp. 69–101.

[23]For citations in this section, see Petracca, "Do Term Limits 'Rob Voters of Democratic Rights?' An Evaluation and Response." For further evidence on the incumbency advantage for House members, see Kenneth Jost, "Term Limits," *Congressional Researcher* 2 (January 10, 1992): 1–19; Monica Bauer and John Hibbing, "Which Incumbents Lose in House Elections: A Response to Jacobsohn's 'The Marginals Never Vanished,'" *American Journal of Political Science* 33 (February 1989): 262–271; and Douglas Rivers and Morris P. Fiorina, "Constituency Service, Reputation, and the Incumbency Advantage," in *Home Style and Washington Work*, ed. Morris P. Fiorina and David W. Rhode (Ann Arbor, Mich.: University of Michigan Press, 1989), pp. 17–45. For state legislators, see David Breaux and Malcolm Jewell, "Winning Big: The Incumbency Advantage in State Legislative Races," in *Changing Patterns of State in State Legislative Careers*, ed. Gary F. Moncrief and Joel A. Thompson (Ann Arbor, Mich.: University of Michigan Press, 1992), pp. 87–105.

privilege, travel funds, and House television and radio studios) to cultivate their districts." For example, a study by Common Cause showed that of the 406 House incumbents who sought reelection in 1990, 158 were financially unopposed, facing challengers who raised less than half as much as the incumbents; and 37 faced challengers with at least half of the incumbents' campaign resources.

The result? "Challengers with enough money to be competitive," said Fred Wertheimer of Common Cause, "are becoming an endangered species." With the enormous resources available to incumbents, it is little wonder there was a 96 percent congressional reelection rate in 1990. Even though 1992 was supposed to be the year of the "antiincumbent," 88 percent of those members of Congress who stood for reelection won, notwithstanding the largest turnover in the House in more than 45 years. Indeed, as Benjamin Ginsberg and Martin Shefter noted, "The absence of competition in congressional elections—which had once characterized only the South—is now becoming a national phenomena."

The advantages of incumbency are increasingly evident throughout all levels of American politics. The professionalization of state legislatures during the past three decades has led to an equally sharp decline in legislative turnover and electoral competition. "Combining all types of legislatures [shows that the average] turnover in each chamber is now less than half what it was in the 1930s," observed Alan Rosenthal. A "new breed" of professional legislator, "who wants to stay in public office for the long haul," increasingly dominates state legislatures.

Term-limits critics dispute the accuracy and implications of this analysis.[24] First, critics note that congressional incumbents have always been disproportionately successful in seeking reelection going back to 1790. On only seven occasions have reelection rates for the House fallen below 70 percent and frequently (81 out of 103 times) they have exceeded 80 percent.

Fair enough. The problem is, throughout most of the nineteenth century not very many members of Congress sought reelection! Not until 1901, for example, did the average number of terms served by

---

[24]The most careful critiques can be found in Morris P. Fiorina, *Divided Government* (New York: Macmillan Publishing Co., 1992) and G. Calvin MacKenzie, L. Sandy Maisel, and Lisa B. Prenaveau, "Congressional Term Limits: Predictable Impacts, Unintended Consequences," Paper presented to the Annual Meeting of the New England Political Science Association, Providence, R.I., April 4, 1992.

House members prior to the present session rise above two terms. There were a few occasions in which the average length of service approached two terms, but not more than a handful out of some 56 sessions. In the twentieth century the average number of terms in the House has been rising steadily. The average number of terms served by members of Congress was 6.2 for the 102nd Congress and is down slightly to 5.3 in the 103rd.[25] Yet notwithstanding similar reelection rates for nineteenth and twentieth century members of Congress, there's a big difference between members of Congress who serve fewer than 4 years before returning to private station and those who serve more than 10.

Term-limits advocates also lament the dramatic decline in turnover in the House. During the 25 elections between 1850 and 1898, for example, turnover averaged 50.2 percent. On average, more than half the House during any given session in the second half of the nineteenth century was made up of first-term members. Conversely, for the last 25 elections, going back to 1944, turnover has averaged only 16.1 percent.[26] For the last fifty years only one out of every six members of the House in a new session of Congress has been a first-term member. Term-limits critics grudgingly concede that "by the standards of congressional history, turnover has been diminished," though they hasten to add, "at least marginally."[27] If the difference between an average turnover rate of 50.2 percent and 16.1 percent is "marginal," it's little wonder political scientists have difficulty understanding the public's embrace of term limits.

Next, term-limits critics argue that congressional turnover is still significant, though it takes time to occur. "Between 1974 and 1982 the membership of the House and Senate was almost entirely replaced as a result of retirements and incumbent defeats," says Thomas Mann. "By the early 1980s three-fourths of senators and representatives had served fewer than 12 years. That tumultuous decade in congressional elections was followed by the placid years after 1982, which saw a

[25]See Stuart A. Rice, *Quantitative Methods in Politics* (New York: Russell & Russell, 1928); and Norman J. Ornstein, Thomas E. Mann, and Michael J. Malbin, *Vital Statistics on Congress, 1993–1994* (Washington, D.C.: CQ Press, 1993).

[26]Calculated from George Will, *Restoration: Congress, Term Limits and the Recovery of Deliberative Democracy* (New York: The Free Press, 1992), p. 73 and Ornstein, Mann, and Malbin, *Vital Statistics*, p. 58.

[27]MacKenzie, Maisel, and Prenaveau, "Congressional Term Limits," p. 7.

drop in voluntary retirements and election defeats and therefore a much more stable membership."[28]

Mann's description of this period is problematic. Even if we accept the proposition that between 1974 and 1982 the membership of the House and Senate was "almost entirely replaced," the real question is *how* were they replaced—as a consequence of retirement or through electoral competition? It turns out that 56 percent retired and 44 percent were defeated in an election. While voluntary retirement by members of Congress is to be applauded as consistent with the rotative principle, it's not the way one would expect turnover to occur if there were truly competitive elections.

Moreover, Mann claims that by the early 1980s three-fourths of representatives and senators had served fewer than 12 years. This just isn't accurate, at least not according to the data compiled by Ornstein, Mann, and Malbin in *Vital Statistics on Congress*. The percentage of House members serving for 14 years or more (7 or more terms) was 25 percent in 1981 and 24 percent in 1983. Think about it. Unless there were no members of Congress having previously served 12 or 13 years in the House, the percentage serving "fewer than 12 years" could not possibly have reached the three-fourths level asserted by Mann. In 1981 and 1983 it would be *accurate* to say three-fourths served fewer than 14 years—but not "fewer than 12 years." Since 1985 the percentage of House members serving longer terms is again on the rise, with an average of 32 percent serving 14 years or more.

The same analysis is true for the Senate. Three-fourths of the Senate served for 12 or fewer years only in 1981 when 25 percent had served 13 or more years. Yet, during this "tumultuous period" of congressional turnover, 1973-1983, an average of 33 percent of the Senate were serving for 13 or more years. More significantly, 18 percent of the Senate were serving 19 or more years on average during the same great period of turnover. As with the House, the percentage of senators serving 13 or more years has risen again during the last five elections, averaging 41 percent of the Senate. Despite all the fuss made over the historic turnover in the 1992 election, 53 members of the Senate in the 103rd Congress have served

[28]Thomas E. Mann, "The Wrong Medicine," *The Brookings Review* 10 (Spring 1992): 24.

for 13 or more years (with 21 having served for 19 or more years). This is the most "senior" Senate in Congress for more than 40 years!

Yes, turnover in the House and Senate takes place, after all even long-term incumbents eventually retire or pass away. Occasionally someone even loses an election. But if it takes more than a decade to achieve what nineteenth century members of Congress did in two or three terms, turnover is too little, too slow to preserve liberty, promote citizen participation, and enhance political representation.

There is one additional point about the permanent legislature that term-limits critics do not discuss. Members of both the House and Senate, *want* to build legislative careers in Congress. A study of the 100th Congress by the Center for Responsive Politics asked members of Congress how long they would "like to stay on Capitol Hill." Only 13 percent of House and 15 percent of Senate members said they were interested in staying in office for 12 years or fewer. More than 50 percent of House members said they were either interested in staying "20 years or more" or "indefinitely." Senators were significantly less ambitious, notwithstanding their much higher average lengths of tenure, with only 19 percnt giving a similar response. Nearly a quarter of the senators responded by saying, "Don't know, will decide with time."[29] Term limits are certainly one way to help members of the Senate overcome their indecision.

The Antidote to the Professionalization of Politics

No longer citizen-legislators, members of Congress have converted the privilege of representing the American people into a lifelong profession. As discussed above, more members of the House and Senate during the last 30-40 years have spent more time in Congress than ever before. They have wanted to pursue elected office as a career and have succeeding at doing so. During the last 40 years, the institution of Congress has been redesigned by its members to facilitate and accommodate the career aspirations of its members at the expense of its representational and legislative responsibilities.[30]

[29]Center for Responsive Politics, *Congress Speakers—A Survey of the 100th Congress* (Washington, D.C.: Center for Responsive Politics, 1988).

[30]Members of Congress have achieved reelection by creating new federal programs that grant wide decisionmaking discretion to the federal bureaucracy, potentially causing a variety of political and policy-specific problems. As a result, constituents with grievances or demands on the Washington establishment approach their congressmen for relief or assistance. Instead of acting as dutiful representatives dedicated

I endorse term limitation primarily as an antidote to the professionalization of legislative politics in America.[31] The professionalization of politics, previously evidenced, is incompatible with the
essence of representative government. Although it may be useful
for society to encourage the development of professional lawyers,
nurses, social scientists, journalists, or physicians, the qualities and
characteristics associated with being a "professional" politician run
counter to the essential requirements of a representative democracy.

At its most basic, the exercise of a profession entails a set of role
relationships between experts and clients in which the professional
is an expert who offers knowledge and judgment to clients. The
culture of professionalism disconnects and distances the professional—whether doctor, attorney, accountant, or politician—from
those whom he or she intends to serve. Conversely, representative
government is characterized by the close connection that necessarily
must exist between the representative and represented. It aspires to
minimize, rather than expand, the distance between the two sets
of citizens.

There are differing theories of representation. However, the classic
distinction between the representative as a trustee and as a delegate
(or agent) remains a useful guide to the conceptual boundaries of
representational theory. Trustees depend on their own conscience,
what they think is right, or their considered judgment of the facts
relevant to a particular decision. The representative as delegate must
express the will, and speak the opinions, of the constituents that
depute him or her.

Theory is one thing; representation in practice is something else.
America's Founders were sensitive to the complexity of the concept,
but they also had a commonsense understanding of its essence—
that representation requires the representative to strike a balance
between representing the interests of the constituents and occasionally acting on their behalf. That approach was put simply by

---

to solving local and national problems, they achieve career security by serving constit-
uents as ombudsmen vis-à-vis Washington's burgeoning bureaucratic establishment.
See Morris P. Fiorina, *Congress: Keystone to the Washington Establishment*, 2nd ed. (New
Haven, Conn.: Yale University Press, 1989); and Rivers and Fiorina, "Constituency
Service, Reputation, and the Incumbency Advantage." What is true for Congress
can also be said for a great many of the "professional" state legislatures.

[31]Citations for the rest of this section can be found in Mark P. Petracca, "The Poison
of Professional Politics," *Cato Institute Policy Analysis* 151 (May 10, 1991). A compatible,
though distinctive, appraisal can be found in Will, *Restoration*.

Abraham Lincoln during his reelection campaign to the General Assembly of Illinois: "I shall be governed by their will on all such subjects upon which I have the means of knowing what their will is, and upon all others I shall do what my own judgment teaches me will best advance their interests."

It is significant that, despite so many other profound disagreements, the Federalists and Antifederalists had rather similar operational definitions of representation. The Federalists tilted toward the trustee side of the representational continuum, while the Antifederalists tilted toward the delegate side. Both realized that effective → representation required a shared space—a proximity of sympathy and interests—between representative and represented. While the representative may not be obliged to merely "re-present" constituent instructions, the expectation was that the proximity of sympathy and interests will come close to accomplishing that anyway, even when the representative acts as a trustee.

Whereas representative government aspires to maintain a proximity of sympathy and interests between representative and represented, professionalism creates authority, autonomy, and hierarchy, distancing the expert from the client. This "distancing" has been aptly characterized by Edward H. Crane as "the culture of ruling."[32] Professionalization encourages an independence of ambition, judgments, and behavior that is at odds with the inherently dependent nature of representative government. For representation to resolve that paradox, representatives cannot become experts and constituents cannot be treated as clients. Yet those are precisely the new roles in which representative and represented are cast by the professionalization of legislative politics in America.

As a result, the term professional representation as applied to politics is an oxymoron. The oft-touted expertise of professional politicians as representatives stands in stark contradiction to the essential function of political representation in a democratic republic, namely, to connect the people to the government through representatives who share their values and stay in touch with the reality of their day-to-day lives.

Suspicion of professional representatives is well-advised. They not only pose a threat to the quality of representation in government

[32]Edward H. Crane, "Six and Twelve: The Case for Serious Term Limits," *National Civic Review* (Summer 1991): 248–55.

as previously discussed, but, through the power of incumbency, they restrict the entry of amateurs—citizen-legislators—into the governing process. As the distinguished historian Daniel Boorstin advises: "The representative of the people ... must be wary of becoming a professional politician. The more complex and gigantic our government, the more essential that the layman's point of view have eloquent voices." Today, the layman's voice in the halls of Congress and in too many state capitols has been silenced by a chorus of career legislators and other professional politicians. Since "democracy is government by amateurs," Boorstin warns, "the survival of our society depends on the vitality of the amateur spirit in the United States today and tomorrow."

However, there scarcely is any room left for amateurs in the modern American legislature. "We must find ways to help our representatives preserve their amateur spirit," Boorstin proposes. Appreciating America's experience with the republican principle of rotation in office and its contemporary counterpart, term limitation, may be one way to effectively restore the amateur spirit to legislatures and begin the process of recovering American politics from professional politicians. It's time for all American legislators to be promoted to private station for study at the "university in rotation."[33]

Experience: Crux of the Neo-Hamiltonian Critique

Experience is key to the neo-Hamiltonian critique of term limitation. Without experienced legislators Congress will be much less productive and representative. Absent experienced members, Congress will be ripe for conquest by special interests, staff, bureaucrats, and the executive. This line of criticism appears repeatedly in the writings of term-limits opponents. Consider just a small sample of pertinent criticism:

> **David Price** (political scientist and member of Congress): Term-limits proponents often seem to think that serving in Congress requires no particular experience or expertise, that an assembly composed solely of amateurs could function

---

[33]Ben Franklin, an advocate for rotation in the Presidency and Senate, strongly objected to the argument that rotation degraded those who had served so faithfully: "In free Governments, the rulers are the servants and the people their superiors and sovereigns. For the former, therefore, to return among the latter was not to degrade but to promote them." See Warren, *The Making of the Constitution*, p. 364. The idea of a "university in rotation" comes from John Adams as previously cited.

quite satisfactorily. . . . To do the job satisfactorily and knowledgeably requires a long-term investment by the member and, in a sense, by his or her constituents. . . . As a whole, Congress would lose power [under term limits]. In particular, members of Congress . . . would become less knowledgeable, less seasoned, less confident, and hence more dependent on staff, lobbyists, and bureaucrats for information and advice.

Victor Kamber (Washington-based political consultant): The idealized citizen-politician and its relevance to the contemporary political environment have been grossly overstated by the limiters. . . . Legislatures comprised exclusively of neophytes and trainees would become alarmingly less competent. They would be stripped of the experience, institutional memory, wisdom, and judgment needed to govern effectively. . . . In such circumstances, political power would flow to: legislative staff members; long-time executive branch bureaucrats; and veteran lobbyists, special interests, and advocacy groups. Finally, term limits would result in successive waves of lame-duck legislators—men and women who would . . . have less incentive, especially in their final terms, to be responsible and accountable to their constituents.

Editors of the *New York Times*: By the same token, limits can foster mediocrity, by discouraging men and women genuinely interested in government as a professional calling, not just a brief fling. And by terminating everyone after a fixed number of years, term limits guarantee that permanent professional staff members—bureaucrats elected by no one—will have the real power, conferred by continuity and experience.

Nelson W. Polsby (UC Berkeley political scientist): It seems self-evident that Congress as an institution would function less well under term limits. While time-servers would be automatically eliminated by term limits, so would conscientious legislators, specialists, and other members whose acumen is sharpened by experience. Term limits would cripple the ability of Congress, . . . to do its job properly of legislating and not legislating, appropriating and not appropriating, advising, consenting, and not consenting, checking and balancing, and legitimizing the acts of government. . . . In the end congressional term limits merely empower lobbyists, congressional staff, bureacrats, presidents, journalists, all

those upon whose experience and guidance an inexperienced
Congress would have to depend.[34]

For these and many other critics of term limits, experience is a
necessary condition for effective legislation and representation; its
absence will shift political power to an assortment of other groups
and individuals—staff, lobbyists, bureaucrats, and the executive.

Advancing this line of argument is one thing, but proving it is
another. Of course, in the debate over term limitations, the burden
of proof rests squarely on those advocating a change in the status
quo. Nevertheless, the critics should offer *some* evidence in defense
of these various assertions about the advantages of experience and
the negative consequences of "government by amateurs."

The best evidence the critics have, beyond personal testimonials,
comes from research on congressional careers by John Hibbing of
the University of Nebraska. Hibbing's findings are worth citing
at length:

> Actual involvement in legislative matters (in terms of raw
> activity levels, promoting a focused legislative agenda, and
> shepherding bills through the legislative process) is more
> strongly related to tenure than ever before. No flattening of
> careers is apparent here, despite all the talk about the death
> of apprenticeship. Senior members, more than at any time
> in the last 40 years, are carrying the legislative burden in
> Congress... Tenure in and of itself helps members to be
> involved, legislative players; and this situation definitely did
> not go into abeyance in the 1980s.... On the basis of this
> evidence, mandatory term limitations would seem to be a
> bad idea.[35]

At first glance Hibbing's conclusion is straightforward and seem-
ingly helpful to the opponents of term limits. As tenure increases

[34]See David E. Price, *The Congressional Career* (Boulder, Colo.: Westview Press, 1992),
pp. 162–63; The Kamber Group, "Modern Day Snake Oil: Term Limitations and Why
They Must Be Defeated" (Washington, D.C.: The Kamber Group, October 1991), pp.
20–21; "Term Limits Limit Voters' Rights," *New York Times*, October 21, 1993, p. A–18;
and Nelson W. Polsby, "Some Arguments Against Congressional Term Limitations,"
Harvard Journal of Law and Public Policy 16 (1993): 104.

[35]John R. Hibbing, "Contours of the Modern Congressional Career," *American Political Science Review* 85 (June 1991): 425–26. See also, Hibbing, *Congressional Careers*
(Chapel Hill, N.C.: University of North Carolina Press, 1991).

in Congress so does legislative responsibility and activity. Experience, at least as measured by tenure, is directly connected to the task of legislating. Not everyone agrees with Hibbing's conclusion. Some scholars argue that Congress has become an institution far more open to junior, less-experienced members; others contend new members of Congress have far more legislative experience today than ever before; and still others maintain that despite greater levels of activity associated with tenure in office, the quality of this work as measured in terms of legislative specialization and success is not significantly different.[36]

Taking Hibbing's findings at face value, however, what has he actually discovered? Seniority matters. In an institutional system that allocates perks, position, and power on the basis of time served, more senior members are going to be in a far better position to engage in productive legislative activity. What Hibbing has not shown is that absent the seniority system, tenure in office alone, as a measure of experience, is a key to effectiveness as legislator and representative. Hibbing's research proves that under the rules currently allocating perks, position, and power in the House, a member must have seniority before he or she is able to fully engage the legislative process. It's not experience that leads to greater legislative activity and success, it's tenure in and of itself. Change the possibilities for extended tenure in the House and the seniority system will disappear. When extended tenure is no longer possible, legislative activity and success will not be a function of how long a member has served in that body.[37]

---

[36]See Burdett A. Loomis, "Congressional Careers and Party Leadership in the Contemporary House of Representatives," *American Journal of Political Science* 28 (1984): 180–202; Gary W. Copeland, "Seniority and Committee Transfers: Career Planning in the Contemporary House of Representatives," *Journal of Politics* 49 (May 1987): 553–64; Michael Berkman, "State Legislative Professionalization and the Congressional Career Path," Paper presented at the Annual Meeting of the Midwest Political Science Association, Chicago, April 16–18, 1993; and Michael K. Moore and Sunil Ahuja, "On Tenure and Legislative Behavior in the U.S. Senate: Examining a Fundamental Assumption of the Term Limits Debate," Unpublished paper, September 1993.

[37]On this and other ways in which term limits will positively change the incentives for representational and legislative behavior, see Amihai Glazer and Martin P. Wattenberg, "Promoting Legislative Work: A Case for Term Limits," Paper presented at the Conference on Term Limits, University of California at Irvine, Irvine, Calif., May 31–June 1, 1991.

But the neo-Hamiltonian criticism of term limits should not be put to rest so easily. Other important responses to this critique are worth mentioning as well.

First, legislative experience is certainly important, but the critics assume new members of Congress will be utterly lacking in it. This is an unfounded assumption. Studies show an increasing number of new members of the House have experience as a result of prior service in state legislatures. Moreover, the time it takes someone serving in the House to gain the knowledge and experience necessary to be an effective representative and legislator is grossly exaggerated.[38] Term-limits critics would have us believe that either members of Congress are slow learners or that Congress is such a complicated institution that for the first three or four terms members are basically worthless to the nation as legislators and/or to their constituents as representatives.

Second, there are other kinds of experience missing from professionalized legislatures. In a study of state legislatures, Peverill Squire found that the level of professionalization is negatively related to the proportion of women serving in office and to the degree of occupational diversity.[39] Term limits will change this as evidenced in a study of California's Assembly Class of '92, the first group of legislators elected after the passage of Proposition 140. According to Charles Price:

> First, the class is divided almost equally among men and women and party. Second, about one-fifth of the class is Latino and for the first time in 12 years an Asian-American has been elected to the lower House. Significantly, given that any connection to the Legislature was a liability in 1992, only two new members came from former legislative staff—a marked departure from the trend in recent elections when many staffers followed their bosses into seats on the floor.[40]

Professional legislatures may actually discourage certain individuals with different kinds of experience from running for office by the

[38]See Berkman, "State Legislative Professionalization and the Congressional Career Path," and Herbert B. Asher, "The Learning of Legislative Norms," *American Political Science Review* 67 (June 1973): 499–513.

[39]Peverill Squire, "Legislative Professionalization and Membership Diversity in State Legislatures," *Legislative Studies Quarterly* 17 (February 1992): 69–79.

[40]Charles M. Price, "Class of '92: The Proposition 140 Babies," *California Journal* (April 1993): 35–36.

very length of time it takes to achieve a position of importance as a legislator. W. Robert Reed and D. Eric Schansberg have developed a model for simulating the quantitative impact of term limits on decisions individuals will make to serve in a term-limited legislature. They find that since term limits will reduce the time that representatives would need to acquire before becoming eligible for leadership positions in the House, "It is not unreasonable that many [other persons] will find service in the U.S. House to be more attractive under term limits." Moreover, in direct contradiction to claims about declining productivity and performance under term-limited legislatures, Reed and Schansberg conclude: "Our findings suggest that term limits might actually improve performance."[41]

Third, experience is not always as good as the advertisement. Though "conventional wisdom holds that the safer lawmakers are, the more willing and able they are to take risks and to cast unpopular votes, the reality, in the contemporary period is the opposite," explains Norman Ornstein. "The safer are the seats in the House, the more skittish are the members. Changes that would bring more competition to House elections would help break this pattern."[42] Electoral safety, which tends to increase with tenure, does not necessarily increase the courage of House members to make difficult decisions or votes. By enhancing competition, term limits may change the incentives of legislators to spend more time legislating and less time servicing constituents.

In addition, what are members of Congress experienced at? James Payne's study, *The Culture of Spending*, shows that the more senior members of Congress are more experienced (and good) at spending taxpayer dollars than are their junior colleagues.[43] If expanding the size of the federal government and the federal deficit were an agreed-upon universal good, then perhaps an attack on seniority through term limits would be ill-advised. But that is hardly the case.

Fourth, contrary to charges that term-limited legislators will slack off in their responsibilities as legislators and representatives when they become "lame-ducks," there is a substantial body of research

[41]W. Robert Reed and D. Eric Schansberg, "An Analysis of the Impact of Congressional Term Limits," Unpublished paper, 1994, forthcoming in *Economic Inquiry*, p. 12.

[42]Norman Ornstein, "The Permanent Democratic Congress," *The Public Interest* 100 (Summer 1990): 43.

[43]James Payne, *The Culture of Spending* (San Francisco: Institute for Contemporary Studies, 1991).

suggesting that last-term "shirking behavior" in Congress is minimal. As John Lott and Stephen Bronars conclude in a recent study of the House: "We find no evidence of economically significant last-term effects on voting behavior, nor are there important effects of legislative tenure on voting patterns."[44]

Fifth, the neo-Hamiltonian critique takes for granted the inability of political amateurs to be effective legislators. This simply isn't the case. In the first definitive study of political amateurs in elections and Congress, David Canon concludes, "It is clear that amateurs play an important role in many aspects of the democratic process, especially in areas of policy change. Although some of these points are speculative and require additional research, according to Canon, amateurs have a hand in (1) providing democratic accountability in congressional elections, (2) resisting socialization pressures in the House and Senate, (3) party building, (4) policy change, and (5) institutional change."[45] Canon presents a compelling defense of political amateurs that confirms both the normative views of Daniel Boorstin and the political predictions of term-limits proponents.

One final comment about experience which harkens back to Aristotle and the response to Hamilton's critique of rotation by the Antifederalists. A truly rotative system does not squander legislative experience; it enhances the experience of individual officeholders. The advantage of "ruling and being ruled by turn," comes about when the ruler gains an appreciation of the sympathy and interests pertinent to the ruled and when those who are ruled have a better understanding of the difficulties and challenges faced by rulers holding public office. Experience at ruling and being ruled is therefore a vital ingredient for promoting governability in a democratic republic.

Democratic governance is never easy; in fact it's downright messy and difficult. Rotation won't make governance any easier, but, for

[44]John Lott and Stephen Bronars, "Time Series Evidence on Shirking in the U.S. House of Representatives," *Public Choice* (January 1993): 125–49. Also consult J. Vanbeek, "Does the Decision to Retire Increase the Amount of Political Shirking?" *Public Finance Quarterly* 19 (October 1991): 444–56.

[45]David T. Canon, *Actors, Athletes, and Astronauts: Political Amateurs in the United States Congress* (Chicago: University of Chicago Press, 1990), p. 157. The recent experience with term limits in California suggests that term limits can have positive consequences for policymaking. See Jerry Gillam, "Term Limits Put Assembly 27 on Bipartisan Path," *Los Angeles Times* [Washington Edition], March 15, 1993, pp. B1 and B4.

all the reasons understood by Americans during the seventeenth, eighteenth, and nineteenth centuries, it might just make it safer, more inclusive, and more responsible.

Conclusion

None of this discussion will satisfy the neo-Hamiltonians, nor perhaps should it. In truth, the debate about the impact of term limits on legislators will not be resolved until term limitations have gone into effect and social scientists have adequate time to study their effects. Right now, the best we can do to assess the policy and political consequences of term limits is to rely upon informed speculation, studies of comparable situations, and possible simulations. This makes the debate lively, frustrating, and ultimately indecisive.

However, from the beginning of the movement I've tended to view term limitation differently, not as a battle over predicted effects, but as a debate about the fundamental principles of republican political design. This is one of the reasons I think a better understanding of rotation as a principle and its operation in practice is so important to the contemporary debate about term limits. Constitutional reform, at any level of government, should not be undertaken out of spite, anger, revenge, or frustration. Instead, reform should be undertaken on the basis of principles necessary to enhance the democratic character of the American republic. Term limitation is precisely such a reform.

6. Congressional Term Limits: A Bad Idea Whose Time Should Never Come

Thomas E. Mann

In the last several years term limits have become the preferred vehicle for expressing public frustration and anger with the political system. Citizen initiatives to limit congressional terms have succeeded in all fifteen states where they were on the ballot, most by overwhelming margins. Numerous state and local jurisdictions have voted to limit the terms of their legislators. Public opinion polls reveal overwhelming popular support for term-limits proposals. If our Constitution could be amended by national initiative, I have no doubt that term limits would soon be enshrined in the fundamental charter of our democracy.

Fortunately, however, we enjoy a representative system of government that requires a level of deliberation before our basic democratic rules can be altered. We are forced to stop and think before acting. Precious little reasoned discussion has accompanied the debates over term limits in the states. Advocates have skillfully tapped the reservoir of public distrust of politicians and stimulated visceral reactions in favor of term limits. Opponents of term limits have largely abdicated their responsibility for joining the debate. Many politicians, fearful of arguing against a proposal that appears to enjoy such broad popular support and of embracing a position that is transparently self-serving, have removed themselves from the fray, trusting that one way or another the term-limits movement will be stopped before its objective is achieved. This myopia has produced a one-sided debate and increased the probability that term limits will someday soon be applied to members of Congress.

I welcome a thoughtful public discussion of congressional term limits—what they are designed to achieve, what their consequences

This paper is adapted from testimony prepared by the author for a November 19, 1993, hearing on congressional term limits before the Subcommittee on Civil and Constitutional Rights, Committee on the Judiciary, U.S. House of Representatives.

might be, and whether more effective remedies might be available for dealing with the problems identified by term-limits advocates. During this debate it is important to remember that the burden of proof—diagnosing the problem and demonstrating that the cure is likely to work without debilitating side effects—properly falls on those who would alter the constitutional order.[1] My view is that a persuasive case for term limits has not been made. What I intend to do here is review and assess that case, based on my reading of an extensive scholarly and popular literature as well as on my own research on congressional elections and congressional reform.

Careerism

The crux of the case for term limits is a rejection of professionalism in politics—or legislative careerism. Careerism is seen as fostering in members of Congress an exclusive focus on reelection and power and a devaluation of the public interest. Advocates see rotation as a way to cure these ills, by preventing a concentration of political power and enhancing government by amateurs—selfless citizens who temporarily answer their country's call to legislate in the public interest.[2] In support of this, they point to the extensive American experience with rotation in office as well as the philosophical under-pinnings for rotation expressed in the founding period, particularly by the Antifederalists.[3]

Most advocates of term limits embrace a conception of democracy that is plebiscitary in character. This conception involves a series of related assertions: Representation is a necessary evil that works only if elected officials closely mirror the instincts and wishes of their constituents. Careerism breeds an arrogance among officeholders that insulates them from the concerns of the people. A permanent political elite turns a deaf ear on the citizens it is elected to serve and pursues its own self-interested agenda.

---

[1]I believe the efforts to limit congressional terms by state initiative will be judged unconstitutional by the Supreme Court, necessitating a constitutional amendment to achieve the desired objective.

[2]John Fund and James Coyne, *Cleaning House: America's Campaign for Term Limits* (Washington, D.C.: Regnery Gateway, 1992).

[3]Mark P. Petracca, "Rotation in Office: The History of an Idea" in *Limiting Legislative Terms*, ed. Gerald Benjamin and Michael J. Malbin (Washington, D.C.: CQ Press, 1992), pp. 19–51.

However, one prominent proponent of term limits, George Will, argues that legislative careerism produces just the opposite effect: Risk-averse members hypersensitive to public sentiment and unwilling to exercise independent judgment.[4] Will champions term limits as a means of restoring deliberative democracy; his compatriots in the movement prefer to empower the people and revitalize direct democracy. What unites them is a belief that citizen-legislators, by virtue either of their more accurate reflection of public sentiment or their wisdom, independently expressed and untainted by career considerations, will more faithfully pursue policies that term-limits proponents favor, which in most cases means a government that spends, taxes, and regulates less.

Since careerism or professionalism is the central malady term limitation is designed to cure, it is important that the several components of the professionalism critique be evaluated. Were the Founders truly sympathetic to mandatory rotation? Is professionalism damaging to our politics and policymaking? Is professionalism in government avoidable? Will term limits replace professionals with amateurs in Congress? Let me address each of these questions in turn.

Whatever the objections raised by the Antifederalists, the Constitution speaks clearly on the issue of mandatory limits. The Founders directly and unanimously rejected the idea of term limits.[5] After much debate, they concluded that frequent elections would be a sufficient safeguard against abuse by incumbents. Indeed, their strategy was not to deny or negate personal ambition but to channel that ambition to serve the public interest. That required giving members a longer-term stake in the institution so that they might look beyond the public's immediate concerns and in Madison's words "refine

[4]George F. Will, *Restoration: Congress, Term Limits and the Recovery of Deliberative Democracy* (New York: The Free Press, 1992).

[5]In his recent testimony before the House Subcommittee on Civil and Constitutional Rights and in an affidavit on the constitutionality of a limit on congressional terms adopted by the state of Washington, Mark Petracca argued that members of the Constitutional Convention never had an opportunity to consider term limits because the measure was not reported out by the Committee on Detail. In point of fact, the Committee of the Whole considered the question of term limits for the legislature on June 12, 1787, and unanimously agreed to strike out the following words: "to be incapable of reelection for the space of [sic] after the expiration of their term of service and to be subject to recall." See Max Farrand, ed., *The Records of the Federal Convention of 1787* (1911; New Haven, Conn.: Yale University Press, 1966), vol. 1, p. 210.

and enlarge" the public view.[6] Will argues rather lamely that a vastly changed political and social situation necessitates trying to restore core values of the Founders' generation by embracing measures that they deemed unnecessary. But Hamilton's words in 1788 ring true today:

> Men will pursue their interests. It is as easy to divert human
> nature as to oppose the strong currents of selfish passions.
> A wise legislator will gently divert the channel, and direct
> it, if possible, to the public good.[7]

What can we say of the costs of professionalism to our politics? Critics of Congress routinely attribute everything they dislike about the institution to careerism. Careerists in Congress are said to be more corrupt, more beholden to special interests, more consumed with pork barrel-projects, more supportive of increased spending, and less responsive to the public interest than amateurs would be.

If these claims were true, we would expect that to be revealed by differences in the behavior of more and less professional legislators. We can search for these differences by comparing junior and senior members in the contemporary Congress. We can compare the behavior of the more professionalized twentieth-century Congress to the more amateur nineteenth-century Congress. We can compare amateur and professional legislatures across countries, states, and localities. None of these comparisons shows that professional legislators are more corrupt, parochial, or influenced by interest groups than their amateur counterparts.[8]

---

[6]This argument is cogently summarized by Michael Malbin, "Federalists v. Antifederalists: The Term-Limitation Debate at the Founding" in Benjamin and Malbin, pp. 53–56.

[7]From the 1788 New York state ratifying convention and quoted in Benjamin and Malbin, pp. 55–56.

[8]Term-limits supporters have relied heavily on James L. Payne's *The Culture of Spending* (San Francisco: ICS Press, 1991) for empirical support of their case that careerism breeds parochialism and excessive spending. While Payne is an unabashed critic of government spending, his study provides little solace for his champions. His own data (Table 5.1, p. 82) reveal that congressional tenure (number of terms served) has a minor effect on spending decisions, one that is swamped by the effects of party and ideology. Moreover, Payne explicitly rejects the pork-barrel theory of congressional elections that is an article of faith among most proponents of term limits as well as citizens who find them so appealing.

Instead, careful study of Congress and every other sector of society suggests that greater professionalism is a necessary offshoot of the growth and specialization of the modern world. If the political rules are rewritten to make it impossible to build a career in Congress, then the institution will have to rely on the professionalism of others to do its job, whether they are staff members, bureaucrats, or lobbyists. The revolt against professionalism is part of a broader populist resentment of elites in all spheres of society and a nostalgia for a bygone Golden Era. But advocates of term limits are hard pressed to offer any examples of amateurism operating successfully in contemporary society, in the United States or abroad. George Will got it right the first time when he wrote: "The day of the 'citizen legislator'—the day when a legislator's primary job was something other than government—is gone. A great state cannot be run by 'citizen legislators' and amateur administrators."[9]

Finally, there is the critical issue of whether term limits would succeed in replacing career politicians with citizen-legislators and whether the latter would fit the image sketched by term-limits proponents. The precise form of the term limits would have a bearing on this question: Simple limits on continuous service in one house would have a very different effect on candidate recruitment from a lifetime limit on service in Congress. The former is likely to foster a class of itinerant professionals who move up and within a hierarchy of term-limited legislatures, no less engaged in the profession of politics, but probably less committed to the larger purposes of the institution of which they are a part. The latter, depending upon the severity of the limit, would alter recruitment patterns; but would the average member fit the image of the disinterested citizen-legislator? I think not.

Absent other changes in the legal and political context of congressional elections, the enormous costs—personal and financial—of running for Congress would not diminish under term limits. Candidate-centered, media-dominated, weak-party campaigns require entrepreneurial skills and resources that are not evenly distributed across American society. Removing the possibility of developing a legislative career would skew the membership of Congress even farther in the direction of a social and economic elite. As political scientist Morris Fiorina has observed, "Amateur political settings

[9]George F. Will, *Statecraft as Soulcraft* (New York: Simon & Schuster, 1983), p. 16.

87

advantage the independently wealthy, professionals with private practices, independent business people, and others with similar financial and career flexibility."[10] Moreover, Syracuse University professor Linda Fowler is almost certainly correct in arguing that patterns of recruitment and forced retirement under term limits will increase the influence of special interests in the legislature.[11]

In sum, the linchpin of the case for term limits—the desirability and feasibility of ending legislative careerism and returning to the citizen legislature originally conceived by the Founders—fails in every key dimension. Mandatory rotation destroys the primary incentive used by the Federalists in writing the Constitution to nurture a deliberative democracy. The perceived ills of contemporary American government—from policy deadlock to pork-barrel spending—have little connection to careerism in Congress. Professionalism is an essential feature of a complex and specialized world. Finally, any effort to use term limits to replace careerists with citizen-legislators is likely to produce some combination of musical chairs by professional politicians with weak institutional loyalties and of participation by elite amateurs with sufficient resources and connections to make a brief stint in Congress possible and profitable.

Competition and Turnover

Another crucial argument advanced on behalf of congressional term limits is the need to restore electoral competition and turnover to a body in which incumbents exploit the advantages of their office to ensure automatic reelection and perpetuate a permanent Congress. Term limits, it is argued, will reinvigorate democracy by leveling the playing field between incumbents and challengers, preventing dynasties from forming in Congress, and guaranteeing that fresh blood and new ideas reach Washington on a regular basis.

There is much to be said for that critique of congressional elections. My colleague at Brookings, Bill Frenzel, a former Republican member of the House from Minnesota, developed the argument in a

[10]Morris P. Fiorina, "Divided Government in the States" in *The Politics of Divided Government*, ed. Cary W. Con and Samuel Kendall (Boulder, Colo.: Westview Press, 1991), pp. 192–93.

[11]Linda L. Fowler, "A Comment on Competition and Careers" in Benjamin and Malbin, pp. 181–85.

recent article in *The Brookings Review*.[12] I responded to Frenzel's argument in an accompanying essay.[13] I urge interested parties to review carefully our respective assertions and evidence. Here I will simply summarize what I see as the major problems with that argument for term limits.

One concern of critics can easily be put to rest. There is no permanent Congress. Indeed, it is ludicrous that the term continues to be used following the 1992 elections, which produced the largest turnover in the House since 1948. Many analysts overgeneralized from the quiescent House elections between 1984 and 1988. The fact is that the membership of the House and Senate is largely remade every decade. The years between 1974 and 1982 produced a high level of turnover from retirements and incumbent defeats. By the early 1980s three-fourths of senators and representatives had served fewer than 12 years. Membership stabilized during the rest of the decade as new members settled in and the public showed little interest in throwing the rascals out. That pattern began to change in 1990, although a weak field of challengers kept House incumbent losses to fifteen members in spite of the widespread signs of public discontent. But 1992 confirmed that we are once again in a period of rapid membership turnover. Every indication is that high levels of voluntary retirement and incumbent defeat will continue in 1994.

While achieving a healthy flow of new blood is not a serious problem for the House or Senate, ensuring a reasonable level of competition is. Incredibly high reelection rates and large margins of victory (more so in the House than in the Senate) are a legitimate concern. But term limitations are unlikely to increase the competitiveness of congressional elections. Increased competition requires more high-quality, well-financed challengers, but term limits would neither materially reduce the disincentives to running for Congress nor increase the effectiveness of party recruiting mechanisms. Potential candidates would continue to weigh the disruptions to family life and career, loss of privacy, demands of fundraising, and the other unpleasantness of modern campaigns. Moreover, there is no reason to believe that term-limited incumbents would be any less

[12]Bill Frenzel, "Term Limits and the Immortal Congress: How to Make Congressional Elections Competitive Again," *The Brookings Review* (Spring 1992): 18–22.

[13]Thomas E. Mann, "The Wrong Medicine: Term Limits Won't Cure What Ails Congressional Elections," *The Brookings Review* (Spring 1992): 23–25.

determined to retain their seats for the full period permitted by the amended Constitution. The odds of a challenger's defeating an incumbent would not increase under term limits. Indeed, a term limit would very likely turn into a floor, with would-be candidates deferring their challenges and awaiting the involuntary retirement of the incumbent. If a norm of deference to term-limited incumbents took root, elections would be contested only in open seats, and then only those not safe for one political party or the other. This would mean a net reduction in the competitiveness of congressional elections.

One important (though usually unstated) target of term-limits proponents is the permanent majority status of the House Democratic party. Presumably Republicans would have a better chance of climbing out of the minority if the cohort of veteran Democratic legislators were forced to give up their seats without a fight. I am sympathetic to the goal—an occasional change in the House majority party in line with national political tides would be good for politics and governance—but dubious of the means. Yet during the 1980s, while Republicans fared better in open seats than in those contested by an incumbent, even here their performance fell short of the Democrats'. Term limits just won't get the job done, whether the job is increasing competition generally or elevating the Republicans to majority status. The right responses are more targeted interventions to build a stronger Republican "farm team" of candidates, to put more resources into the hands of challengers and limit the material advantages of incumbency, and to raise the national stakes in congressional elections.

Accountability

Another argument advanced by term-limits supporters, one that is related to the critique of careerism, is that members of Congress are not genuinely accountable to the people who send them to Washington. The overriding goal of reelection leads members to pursue a manipulative relationship with their constituents—they buy safe districts by shoveling pork and catering to special interests with access to campaign resources. Ordinary citizens are anesthetized and potential challengers discouraged, thereby allowing members to pursue their own agendas in Washington without any realistic fear that they will be held to account for their actions.

There are grounds for concern here. Uncontested elections and halfhearted challenges are unlikely to have a bracing effect on incumbents and over time may breed an unhealthy feeling of invulnerability and arrogance. Moreover, heavy investments in constituent service tend to depoliticize the relationship between representatives and constituents and minimize the possibility of policy accountability. Yet most members of Congress remain unbelievably insecure about their political futures and highly responsive to the interests of their constituencies. One major reason incumbents are so successful is that electoral accountability is alive and well: Representatives conform to the wishes of their constituents and are in turn rewarded with reelection.

The problem is not individual accountability. Voters show no signs of suffering from inattentive or unresponsive representatives. If anything, members of Congress are too solicitous of their constituencies and insufficiently attentive to broader national interests, too consumed with their personal standing in their district or state, and too little dependent on their political party.

What many of us sense is in short supply in the contemporary Congress is a collective accountability that provides an appropriate balance between local and national interests, between narrow and general interests, and between short-term preferences and long-term needs. The present system appears to favor local, special, and immediate interests over national, general, and future concerns. Will believes the way to right that balance and to restore congressional deliberation in service of the public interest is to remove members of Congress from the unseemly and demeaning business of elections, to proscribe ambition in public life rather than to channel it, and to take the politics out of government.

I believe this effort is self-defeating. It would deny the democratic connection rather than revitalize it. There is simply no reason to believe that a term-limited Congress would be more accountable to the American people or that it would be more inclined to advance the public interest. If anything, term limitations are likely to shift the focus of members of Congress even more in the direction of local and immediate concerns.

Congressional Organization and Power

The final argument offered by proponents is that term limits would transform the institution of Congress, making it more productive, more deliberative, less dependent on staff and special interests, less disposed to micromanage programs and agencies, and better structured to reward members on the basis of ability rather than seniority. As I understand the logic of this argument, term limits would change the motivations of legislators and subsequently their behavior by removing the incentive to put reelection and personal power within the chamber above other considerations, such as making public policy in the national interest.

It requires an extraordinary leap of faith to believe that term limits will produce these desirable institutional changes, especially in light of my earlier discussion of the electoral effects of term limits. We have no direct evidence on which to rely—term limitations have been in effect in the states for too brief a time to provide an empirical basis for any reliable generalizations. Indeed, there is much to be said for taking advantage of our federal system by assessing the state experiments with term limits before enshrining them in the U.S. Constitution. A number of very interesting scholarly studies are now being launched and pertinent findings will begin to emerge as state term limits take effect over the next several years. But I suspect my call for experimentation and deliberation will not mollify leaders of the term-limits movement.

Absent any reliable evidence, I simply note that the institutional changes mentioned above do not logically follow from the imposition of term limits. Take legislative productivity. As Michael Malbin and Gerald Benjamin have observed, a legislature of well-meaning amateurs, determined to decide on the merits of an issue unsullied by career considerations, has no guarantee of success. While critics often attribute stalemate to cowardly politicians unwilling to make tough decisions, it more often occurs among legislators who want to do the right thing but disagree over what the right thing is.[14]

Or take deliberation, which George Will sees as occurring in a legislature where "members reason together about the problems confronting the community and strive to promote policies in the general interest of the community."[15] Ironically, the term-limits movement is the very antithesis of deliberation. It is riding the crest of a plebiscitary wave in our politics which favors initiatives,

[14]Michael J. Malbin and Gerald Benjamin, "Legislatures After Term Limits" in Benjamin and Malbin, p. 211.

[15]George F. Will, *Restoration*, p. 110.

92

referendums, and other forms of direct democracy over the reasoned discussion insulated from public passions preferred by Will. I find it hard to imagine how term limits would foster deliberation in Congress. Members would continue to have a reelection incentive until they came up against the limit. A greater impatience to build a record of achievement would not necessarily augur well for the national interest; short-sighted solutions to immediate problems could just as easily be the result.

More importantly, the intense individualism of the contemporary Congress would be strengthened, not weakened, under term limits. There would be little incentive for members to follow the lead of others, be they party leaders or committee chairmen. The elimination of seniority as a basis for leadership selection, a likely consequence of term limits, would intensify competition and conflict among members but devalue the authority of those positions. Few rewards and resources would exist for institutional maintenance and policy leadership—protecting the independence and integrity of Congress, setting legislative agendas, and mobilizing majorities. With little change in the media and interest group environment of Congress, the centrifugal forces in Congress would remain strong while the centralizing instruments would be weakened.

Much the same can be said for the other improvements in the institutional performance of Congress that allegedly would flow from term limits. Term-limited members could prove to be more dependent on special interests for campaign funds, information, and a job after service in Congress than are present members. Less experienced members would perforce rely more heavily on congressional staff and executive branch officials.

Indeed, the more one examines the claims of term-limits advocates, the more one is struck by the utter failure of advocates to make a convincing case connecting remedies with problems. If Congress were to legislate in a complex policy area on the basis of theories and evidence no better than I have summarized here, it would be roundly (and properly) criticized by many of those who now embrace term limits. There is, I believe, no substantive case for amending the U.S. Constitution to limit the terms of members of the House and Senate.

While I believe the failure of proponents to present a convincing argument for term limits is sufficient reason for rejecting a constitutional amendment, there are two additional reasons for resisting popular sentiment on this issue.

Democracy

Term limits would diminish our democracy by restricting it unnecessarily. Voters now have the power to end the career of their representatives and senators by the simple exercise of the franchise. At present they also enjoy the power to retain in office those officials whom they believe merit reelection. The Constitution properly precludes the citizens of one district or state from limiting the electoral choice of those residing somewhere else.

I fully support efforts to increase the supply of able, well-financed challengers and to enhance the quality and quantity of relevant information about incumbents available to citizens. Such steps would increase the competitiveness of congressional elections and expand the choices available to voters. But an arbitrary limit on terms of congressional service is an antidemocratic device masquerading as the champion of democratic revival.

The Founders said it best, as Chief Justice Warren noted in his 1944 decision in *Powell v. McCormack*: "A fundamental principle of our representative democracy is, in Hamilton's words, 'that the people should choose whom they please to govern them' [2 Elliot's debates 257]. As Madison pointed out at the convention, this principle is undermined as much by limiting whom the people can select as by limiting the franchise [itself]."[16]

Experience

Longevity and experience do not correspond perfectly with wisdom and effectiveness. Some incumbents overstay their productive periods in Congress and are treated too generously by their constituents at reelection time. Every legislative body needs regular infusions of new members to reflect changing public sentiments and to put new ideas into the legislative process. Opportunities should exist for junior members to participate meaningfully in the legislative process.

---

[16]*Powell v. McCormack*, 395 U.S. 486, 547 (1969).

That being said, I believe it would be a terrible mistake to end all careers in Congress after six or twelve years.[17] Legislative talent—which encompasses among other traits a respect for the public, a capacity to listen to people who disagree with you, bargaining skills, a willingness to compromise, an appreciation for parliamentary procedure, and a capacity to move easily between technical knowledge and ordinary experience—is not in overabundant supply. Able people must be encouraged to make substantial investments in developing these skills and applying them on behalf of the public interest. Anyone familiar with the current Congress can name dozens of senior members in both parties whose careers defy the stereotype of term-limits supporters. They have serious policy interests, they are legislative workhorses, they have the confidence to resist temporary passions and interest-group pressures, and they demonstrate a respect for their institution and the pivotal role it plays in the American constitutional system. History is filled with examples of legislative careerists who made substantial contributions to their country, including such notables as Robert LaFollette, Jr., Arthur Vandenberg, Edmund Muskie, and Sam Ervin. Term limits would have ended their careers in Congress before they made their mark. Rather than demonstrate contempt for such careers, we should think about how we might encourage others to make a comparable investment.

Conclusion

Term limitation is a false panacea, a slam-dunk approach to political reform that offers little beyond emotional release of pent-up frustrations with the performance of the economic and political system. Shortcomings in the electoral process and in the organization of Congress should be dealt with directly, in ways that strengthen representative democracy and the institution closest to the people.[18]

---

[17]John R. Hibbing has provided the most systematic evidence linking congressional tenure with legislative effectiveness: "Senior members are the heart and soul of the legislative side of congressional service." *Congressional Careers* (Chapel Hill: University of North Carolina Press, 1991), p. 126.

[18]An agenda for congressional reform is presented in Thomas E. Mann and Norman J. Ornstein, *Renewing Congress: A First Report* (Washington, D.C.: AEI and Brookings, 1992) and *Renewing Congress: A Second Report* (Washington, D.C.: AEI and Brookings, 1993).

PART III

THE LAW OF TERM LIMITS

7. The Constitutionality of State-Imposed Term Limits for Federal Office

Lloyd N. Cutler

The proponents of congressional term limits speak eloquently of the problems that can be posed for the country by an entrenched class of career politicians and are quick to quote the debates surrounding the adoption of our Constitution as support for their cause. However, these proponents often overlook another important feature of the constitutional debates: that after considering term limits and other qualifications for federal office, the Founders agreed upon a final list of qualifications, and determined that they should be exclusive. This was the conclusion of the Supreme Court in *Powell v. McCormack*,[1] and it remains good law today.

The Supreme Court held in *Powell* that the Constitution sets forth an exclusive list of qualifications for service in Congress. The Court articulated that conclusion after an extensive review of the historical record, which reflected that the Constitution's qualifications were intended to be " '*defined* and *fixed*,' "[2] and *immutable*,[3] having been " 'unalterably determined by the Federal Convention.' "[4] Numerous federal courts, including the second, ninth, and eleventh circuits, and most recently in the Western District of Washington, have concluded that *Powell*'s holding is based on the meaning of the Constitution— i.e., the Founders' intent to provide an exclusive list of qualifications—and is thus equally applicable to Congress and the states.[5]

---

[1]395 U.S. 486 (1969).

[2]Ibid., p. 539 (emphasis in original) (quoting the *Federalist*, no. 60).

[3]Ibid., p. 540 (discussing import of "Hamilton's express reliance on the immutability of the qualifications").

[4]Ibid., pp. 542–43 (quoting 17 *Annals of Cong.*, p. 872 (1807)).

[5]See, e.g., *Joyner v. Mofford*, 706 F.2d 1523, 1528–30 (9th Cir.), *cert denied*, 464 U.S. 1002 (1983); *Signorelli v. Evans*, 637 F.2d 853, 858 (2d Cir. 1980); *Public Citizen, Inc. v. Miller*, 813 F. Supp. 821, 831 (N.D. Ga.), *aff'd mem.*, 992 F.2d 1548 (11th Cir. 1993).

In contrast, I am not aware of a single case that reaches the contrary conclusion.

The proposition that states cannot add to the constitutional qualifications is discussed at length in the Court's opinion in *Powell*.[6] One of the most important historical sources relied on in *Powell* was Congress's "post-ratification" view of the qualifications clauses. The Court began by reviewing the 1807 case of Rep. William McCreery, whose seat in the House was challenged because he failed to meet Maryland's statutory qualification of residence within the congressional district. The Court noted that the House Committee of Elections recommended that McCreery be seated, despite his failure to meet the state's qualification, because the qualifications are determined in the Constitution " 'without reserving any authority to the State Legislatures to change, add to, or diminish those qualifications.' "[7] The Court went on to quote the Chairman's explanation of the Committee's decision, emphasizing that " 'neither the State nor the Federal Legislatures are vested with authority to add to [the Constitution's] qualifications, so as to change them.' "[8] Finally, the Court noted that the full House accepted the Committee's reasoning and seated McCreery by a vote of 89 to 18, after extensive consideration—and rejection—of "the power of the states to add to the standing qualifications."[9]

The *Powell* Court clearly agreed with the Committee's reasoning and the House's decision to seat McCreery. More importantly, the Court observed that this example, and others like it,[10] confirmed the conclusion that a member-elect who meets the constitutional qualifications cannot be excluded.[11] These comments clearly convey the *Powell* Court's belief that the states, as well as Congress, are barred from adding to the Constitution's qualifications for elected federal officers. Indeed, the Court characterized the McCreery debate

[6] *Powell*, pp. 542–47 and nn. 78–83.

[7] Ibid., p. 542 (quoting 17 *Annals of Cong.*, p. 871 (1807)).

[8] Ibid., p. 543 (quoting 17 *Annals of Cong.*, p. 872 (1807)).

[9] Ibid.

[10] The Court referred to three other occasions when the House rejected attempts to exclude members-elect because they failed to meet state-imposed qualifications. See ibid., p. 395 n. 79, and numerous other instances where either the House or the Senate resisted attempts to exclude members-elect for other reasons not within the Constitution's qualifications. Ibid.

[11] Ibid., p. 547.

as centering "on the *more narrow* issue of the power of the States to add to the standing qualifications set forth in the Constitution."[12] This undoubtedly suggests that the Court found the issue of the states' power to impose additional qualifications to be an easier question than that of congressional power to add such qualifications, perhaps because of the language in article I, section 5, clause 1, giving Congress the power to judge the qualifications of its members.

Powell is not the only judicial authority that speaks to the power of the states to vary the Constitution's qualifications. Many federal and twenty-one state courts have considered this issue in cases involving the constitutionality of state-imposed term limits or other state-imposed qualifications for federal office. In each and every case that reached the issue, courts arrived at the same conclusion: The states may not add to the qualifications set forth in the Constitution.

Most significant here are the cases in which courts struck down state laws imposing term limits on federal offices, the most recent of which, *Thorsted v. Gregoire*, struck down Washington's term-limits initiative.[13] But courts also have uniformly struck down other state-imposed qualifications, such as laws disqualifying candidates who failed to meet narrower residency requirements;[14] laws disqualifying candidates convicted of felonies;[15] laws disqualifying candidates suspected of disloyalty;[16] and laws disqualifying candidates who are state officials.[17]

[12]Ibid., p. 543 (emphasis added).

[13]See, e.g., *Thorsted v. Gregoire*, 841 F. Supp. 1068 (1994); *Stumpf v. Lau*, 839 P.2d 120, 123 (Nev. 1992); *State ex rel. Santini v. Swackhamer*, 521 P.2d 568 (Nev. 1974); *Hill v. Tucker*, No. 92-6171 (Ark. Cir. Ct., July 29, 1993); see also *Advisory Opinion to the Attorney General*, 592 So.2d 225, 230–31 (Fla. 1991) (Overton, J. and Kogan, J., dissenting) (majority held that challenge to constitutionality of the terms-limits initiative was unripe until the initiative was enacted; dissenting justices reached the merits of the issue and found that the initiative was plainly unconstitutional under *Powell* and *Davis v. Adams*); *Plugge v. McCuen*, 841 S.W.2d 139, 145–150 (Ark. 1992) (Dudley, J., dissenting) (same).

[14]See, e.g., *Dillon v. Fiorina*, 340 F.Supp. 729 (D.N.M. 1972); *Exon v. Tiemann*, 279 F. Supp. 609 (D. Neb. 1968) (three-judge court); *Hellman v. Collier*, 141 A.2d 908 (Md, 1958); *State ex rel. Chavez v. Evans*, 446 P.2d 445 (N.M. 1968); compare *Strong v. Breaux*, 612 So.2d 111, 112 (La. Ct. App. 1992).

[15]See, e.g., *Danielson v. Fitzsimmons*, 44 N.W.2d 484 (Minn. 1950); *State ex rel. Eaton v. Schmahl*, 167 N.W. 481 (Minn. 1918); *Application of Ferguson*, 294 N.Y.S.2d 174, (N.Y. Sup. Ct.), aff'd, 294 N.Y.S.2d 989 (App. Div. 1968); *In re O'Connor*, 17 N.Y.S.2d 758 (N.Y. Sup. Ct. 1940); cf. *United States v. Richmond*, 550 F.Supp. 605 (E.D.N.Y. 1982) (Weinstein, J., dissenting).

Proponents of state-imposed term limits are quick to point out that some so-called resign-to-run statutes, which require state officeholders to resign before running for federal office, have been upheld against qualifications clause challenges. But these cases support my point: such statutes are sustained only where the state is seeking merely to regulate the conduct of state officials while they choose to remain in state office, and does not bar candidates from running so long as they first resign their state offices.[18] Significantly, even these cases are unanimous in concluding that the Constitution precludes a state from imposing an additional qualification for service in Congress.

The judiciary's unanimous interpretation of the qualifications clauses is supported by the overwhelming historical evidence of the Founders' intent. Indeed, it is unusual to find as clear and conclusive an historical record on a constitutional issue as the record regarding the Constitution's qualifications, especially as concerns term limits. While the historical sources make it clear that there were divergent views about whether term limits should be included in the qualifications clauses and whether the Constitution's qualifications should be exclusive, the record is equally clear on how those questions were resolved: the Founders deliberately left term limits out of the qualifications clauses, and expressed their belief that those clauses were exclusive.

Term limitation was a common feature in post-revolutionary American state constitutions. For example, Virginia, Maryland,

[16]See, e.g., *Shub v. Simpson*, 76 A.2d 332 (Md.) (antisubversion declaration requirement unconstitutional), *appeal dismissed*, 340 U.S. 881 (1950); *In re O'Connor*, 17 N.Y.S.2d 758 (N.Y. Sup. Ct. 1940) (disqualification for disloyalty).

[17]See, e.g., *Stack v. Adams*, 315 F. Supp. 1295 (N.D. Fla. 1970) (three-judge court); *State ex rel. Pickrell v. Senner*, 375 P.2d 728 (Ariz. 1962); *Stockton v. MacFarland*, 106 P.2d 328 (Ariz. 1940); *Buckingham v. State ex rel. Killoran*, 35 A.2d 903, 905 (Del. 1944); *Lowe v. Fowler*, 240 S.E.2d 70 (1977); *State ex rel. Handley v. Superior Court* 151 N.E.2d 508 (Ind. 1958); *Richardson v. Hare*, 160 N.W.2d 883, 887–88 (Mich. 1968); *State ex rel. Santini v. Swackhamer*, 521 P.2d 568 (Nev. 1974); *Riley v. Cordell*, 194 P.2d 857 (Okla. 1948); *Ekwall v. Stadelman*, 30 P.2d 1037 (Or. 1934); *In re Opinion of the Judges*, 116 N.W.2d 233 (S.D. 1962); *State ex rel. Chandler v. Howell*, 175 P. 569 (Wash. 1918); *State ex rel. Wettengel v. Zimmerman*, 24 N.W.2d 504 (Wis. 1946); see also *Cobb v. State*, 722 P.2d 1032 (Haw. 1986).

[18]See *Joyner v. Mofford*, 706 F.2d 1523 (9th Cir.), *cert denied* 464 U.S. 1002 (1983); *Signorelli v. Evans*, 637 F.2d 853 (2d Cir. 1980); *Thorsted v. Gregoire*, 841 F.Supp. 1068 (1994); *Adams v. Supreme Court*, 502 F.Supp. 1282 (M.D. Pa. 1980); *Alex v. County of*

South Carolina, North Carolina, Delaware, and Georgia all had limits on the number of consecutive terms a governor could serve.[19] Pennsylvania limited the terms of its governor and its legislators.[20] The Articles of Confederation adopted term limits as well. Delegates to the Confederation Congress could not serve "for more than three years in any term of six years."[21] Maryland, New Hampshire, Pennsylvania, and Vermont imposed additional restrictions on the terms of their delegates to the Confederation Congress.[22]

By the time of the Constitutional Convention, however, there was a growing consensus that term limitation was a failure. Massachusetts considered but rejected term limits in its 1780 constitution.[23] Pennsylvania repealed its term limits in the 1780s, explaining that "the privilege of the people in elections, is so far being infringed as they are thereby deprived of the right of choosing those persons whom they would prefer."[24] The Confederation Congress lost almost its entire delegation from Rhode Island in 1784, apparently because of the term limits in the Articles; this seems to have soured many of the Founders on term limits.[25]

There is no question that the Founders considered and rejected term limits. The Virginia Plan proposed that members of the House and Senate be ineligible for reelection for an unspecified number of years after their terms, and that the President be permanently ineligible for reelection.[26] The Convention, however, voted unanimously to remove congressional term limits from the Virginia Plan.[27] After

---

Los Angeles, 111 Cal. Rptr. 285 (Ct. Ap. 1973); *Oklahoma State Election Board v. Coats,* 610 P.2d 776 (Okla. 1980); see also *State ex rel. Watson v. Cobb,* 2 Kan. 27, 54 (1863).

[19]Md. Const. sec. XXXI (1776); Va. Const. chapt. II, sec. IX (1776); S.C. Const. VI (1778); Del. Const. art. 7 (1776); N.C. Const. XV (1776); Ga. Const. art. XXIII (1777).

[20]Pa. Const. sec. 19 (1776).

[21]Article V.

[22]Brendan Barnicle, Note, "Congressional Term Limits: Unconstitutional by Initiative," *Washington Law Review* 67 (1992): 415, 417.

[23]Gordon S. Wood, *The Creation of the American Republic, 1776–1787* (New York: The Norton Library, 1969), p. 436. See the discussion in *Opinion of the Justices to the Senate,* 595 N.E.2d 292, 298–301 (Mass. 1992).

[24]Gordon S. Wood, *The Creation of the American Republic, 1776–1787,* p. 493.

[25]See Tiffanie Kovarevich, Note, "Constitutionality of Term Limitations: Can States Limit the Terms of Members of Congress?," *Pacific Law Journal* 23 (1992): 1677, 1679–80.

[26]Max Farrand, ed., *The Records of the Federal Convention of 1787* (1911; New Haven, Conn.: Yale University Press, 1966), pp. 20–21 (resolutions 4, 5, and 7).

[27]Ibid., p. 217.

considerable debate, the Convention also voted to remove any term limit on the President.[28]

The debate at the Convention also indicates that the Founders believed that the Constitution's qualifications would be exclusive. For example, in the debate over including a property qualification, Madison opposed the idea of giving Congress the power to impose such a restriction. He argued that the qualifications of legislators were "fundamental articles in a Republican Govt. and ought to be fixed by the Constitution."[29]

Madison noted that, unless fixed in the Constitution, "qualifications founded on artificial distinctions may be devised by the stronger in order to keep out partisans of a weaker faction."[30] Hugh Williamson of North Carolina agreed, arguing that if the qualifications were not fixed in the Constitution and if a majority of some future Congress were lawyers, those qualifications could require that only lawyers could become members of Congress.[31]

The evidence from the ratification debate is also clear. Madison's the *Federalist*, no. 52 decisively demonstrates that the Constitution was understood not to allow the states to impose additional qualifications for elected federal offices. In contrasting qualifications for voters, which were left to the states, with qualifications for federal office, Madison wrote: "The qualifications of the elected being less carefully and properly defined by the State constitutions, and being at the same time more susceptible of uniformity, have been properly considered and regulated by the convention."[32] Hamilton agreed, noting in the *Federalist*, no. 60 that the qualifications in the Constitution are "fixed" and "unalterable."[33]

The Founders' decision to exclude term limits as a qualification became one of the major controversies in the ratification debate.[34] The Antifederalists complained that without term limits, Congress

[28]Ibid., pp. 497–502, 522–25.

[29]Ibid., p. 249–50.

[30]Ibid., p. 250.

[31]Ibid.

[32]*The Federalist*, no. 52, p. 354.

[33]Ibid., p. 409. Hamilton was refuting the argument that the Constitution would favor the wealthy. His argument—that since the Constitution does not permit any property qualification for office, the wealthy could not dominate the federal government—presupposes that neither states nor Congress would be able to add qualifications beyond those in the Constitution.

and the President would become an undemocratic aristocracy.[35] This argument presumed that under the Constitution, the states would not be able to impose term limits on their federal representatives.[36] Never in the debate over ratification did anyone suggest that if the Constitution were ratified, states could impose term limits on their representatives in Congress.[37]

The immediate post-ratification experience also demonstrates that the Founders and the states ratifying the Constitution believed its qualifications to be exclusive. Although virtually all of the states in 1787 imposed property qualifications on state offices,[38] not a single state attempted to impose property qualifications on its members of Congress. Similarly, although four states had imposed term limits on their representatives to the Confederation Congress and half of the states still imposed term limits on some state offices in 1787, not a single state attempted to impose term limits on its members of Congress. By contrast, during the debate in the First Congress over the Bill of Rights, one set of proposed amendments to the U.S. Constitution, which never passed Congress, would have limited representatives to three terms during any eight-year period, and would have reduced senators' terms to one year and limited them to five years of consecutive service in any six-year period.[39] This

[34]Elbridge Gerry, who participated in the Philadelphia Convention, declined to sign the Constitution and became a leading Antifederalist in part because of "the duration and re-eligibility of the Senate" and the failure to impose a term limit on the President. Troy Eid and Jim Kolbe, "The New Anti-Federalism: The Constitutionality of State-Imposed Limits on Congressional Terms of Office," *Denver University Law Review* 69 (1992): 1, 14–15.

[35]Gordon S. Wood, pp. 520–21. See generally chapters 12–13 (discussing the debate over ratification). See also Herbert O. Storing, ed., *The Complete Anti-Federalist* (Chicago: University of Chicago Press, 1981) sec. 2.8.147 (letter of "The Federal Farmer" in support of term limits), sec. 2.9.201 (essay of "Brutus" in support of term limits).

[36]Ibid., sec. 3.11.48 (Dissent of the Minority of the Convention of Pennsylvania, Dec. 18, 1787).

[37]Indeed, throughout the ratification debate, the Antifederalists complained bitterly about the Constitution's dilution of state power. If the Federalists believed that the states retained the power to set term limits or other qualifications for members of Congress, they certainly would have said so in response to this criticism.

[38]See Charles Warren, *The Making of the Constitution* (New York: Barnes and Noble, 1967), pp. 416–17 (listing state property qualifications).

[39]Sula P. Richardson, *Congressional Tenure: A Review of Efforts to Limit House and Senate Service* Vol. 4 (Washington: Congressional Research Service, 1989) (citing *Annals of Congress* 17, p. 790 (1789)).

history confirms the common understanding that only a federal constitutional amendment, not the states acting on their own, could add to the qualifications clause.

The early Congresses also read the qualifications clauses as exclusive. In 1807, in conjunction with the challenge to Representative McCreery, the House defeated by a vote of 92–8 a separate resolution stating that states did have a right to add their own qualifications.[40] The 1834 *Cases of Contested Elections* states that this case "settled that the states have not the right to require qualifications different from, or in addition to, those prescribed by the constitution."[41] The Senate later confirmed the same principle.[42]

Congress faithfully adhered to this principle until after the Civil War. In 1868, the House and Senate each voted to exclude members-elect for giving aid and comfort to the Confederacy.[43] While these actions have been described as taken in "the naked urgency of power" and without doctrinal support,[44] they were no doubt influenced by the impending ratification of the Fourteenth Amendment, which had been proposed by Congress in 1866 and was ratified in 1868. After ratification of the Fourteenth Amendment, Congress largely adhered to its position that the Constitution is the sole permissible source of qualifications. The House in 1870 refused to exclude a Texas representative accused of various criminal acts, and in 1933 refused to exclude a Minnesota representative accused of sending defamatory matter through the mail.[45] These events

[40]*Annals of Congress* 17, pp. 1233, 1237 (1807).

[41]M. St. Clair Clarke and David A. Hall, eds. *Cases of Contested Elections* (Washington: Gales and Seaton, 1834), p. 171. See also Asher B. Hinds, *Precedents of the House of Representatives of the United States* (Washington: Government Printing Office, 1907), sec. 414.

[42]In 1856, the Senate seated Lyman Trumbull of Illinois, despite the fact that under the Illinois state constitution he was ineligible until his term as a state judge was over. The Senate decided that state constitutions could not vary or add to the qualifications in the U.S. Constitution. *Cong. Globe*, 34th Cong., 1st Sess. 547–84 (1856). The Trumbull incident is discussed in detail in *State ex rel. Johnson v. Crane*, 197 P.2d 864, 868–69 (Wyo. 1948). Reviewing the precedents in the House and the Senate, "The Legal Qualifications of Representatives," *American Law Review* 3 (1868): 410, found that it was settled law that a state could not add to or otherwise affect the qualifications of that state's members of Congress.

[43]See *Powell*, p. 485 and n. 81.

[44]Ibid., pp. 543–44.

[45]Ibid., p. 545 n. 83. There were, however, two occasions where the House excluded members-elect on the ground that they practiced polygamy. Ibid.

demonstrate that the early Congresses believed that the Constitution is the sole permissible source of qualifications. Indeed, this belief appears to have continued for quite a while, for up until the past three years even the proponents of term limits have consistently viewed them as requiring a federal constitutional amendment.

Another argument put forth by supporters of state-imposed term limits is that such measures do not offend the Constitution if they are presented as ballot-access restrictions, and not qualifications. An example of such a measure is the initiative recently enacted in the state of Washington, which would have prevented three-term incumbents of the House from declaring candidacy for a fourth term, or even from appearing on the ballot. According to the initiative's proponents, this is not a term limit because there is a theoretical possibility that the incumbent could overcome these limitations and win the election by a write-in vote.

In striking down the Washington initiative, Federal District Court Judge Dwyer found this argument to be entirely without merit. The plain purpose of these measures, however denominated, is not to regulate a congressional race by setting reasonable ground rules that every candidate must follow. Instead, it hobbles a few runners to make sure they lose. A state may not constitutionally do that, just as it may not bar qualified runners from the track.[46] Such a measure clearly imposes a qualification, and is not saved by the fact that it leaves some remote mathematical chance that its goal will not be achieved.

Moreover, any qualification disguised as a mere ballot access measure cannot possibly be justified under the Constitution's narrow grant of authority permitting the states to regulate the "Times, Places and Manner of holding elections." The fallacy of this purported justification is demonstrated by the text of the clause itself, which provides that Congress "may at any time by Law make or alter such Regulations." If the times, places, and manner clause empowers the states to add qualifications, then it must similarly empower Congress—a result that *Powell* explicitly negates. Furthermore, even as a ballot-access measure, the law would be plainly unconstitutional as an attempt to impose a discriminatory and crippling burden on a group of constitutionally-qualified candidates.

[46]*Thorsted v. Gregoire*, 841 F.Supp. 1068 (1994).

It may be that in the final analysis, the adoption of term limits for Congress will be seen as a sound policy choice for the nation. But our Constitution—as drafted by the Founders, ratified by the states and interpreted by the Supreme Court in *Powell*—requires that this choice be made, if at all, through a federal constitutional amendment. No substitute enacted by a state will do.

8. State Term-Limits Laws and the Constitution

John G. Kester

The rise of a class of professional enjoyers of elected office has led, it is widely believed, to a bloated and unresponsive kind of congressional government, far removed from what the people wanted in 1787 and from what they want today. Madison anticipated that because elections for the House of Representatives would come often, "new members . . . would always form a large proportion" of the House of Representatives.[1] That view dominated when the Constitution was written. As an ideal, it was attractive. As a prediction, after a century or two, it turned out to be a flop.[2]

A year ago several states—all of them, not coincidentally, states in which the voters can legislate directly by initiative without going through a legislature—passed laws or constitutional amendments to discourage or restrict, in one way or another, the repeated reelection of representatives and senators (as well as of many state officers). One reaction of incumbents has been to be sure that all proposals for extending term limits nationwide stay bottled up in Congress.

Another has been to run for shelter to the courts. There they and their supporters have urged that state laws addressing the modern problem of congressional incumbency must be, somehow, a violation of the Constitution of the United States. So, for example, Thomas Foley, the Speaker of the House, has actually sued the officials of his own state of Washington, claiming that its voters had no power to pass their new law that will keep long-time incumbents off the ballot. Foley laments that although it applies to no election until 1998, it already leaves him "weakened" in his "ability to protect the

---

[1]Max Farrand, ed., *The Records of the Federal Convention of 1787* (1911; New Haven, Conn.: Yale University Press, 1966), vol. 1, p. 361.

[2]See generally George F. Will, *Restoration: Congress, Term Limits and the Recovery of Deliberative Democracy* (New York: The Free Press, 1992), pp. 73–91.

interests of the constituents who elected me and to exercise leadership among my fellow Democrats in the House of Representatives."[3]

The losers at the term-limits ballot box, when they turn to litigation to fight the voters' laws, are embarrassed to find that the Constitution is silent on the subject. Constitutional silence, when Congress has not acted, traditionally has been taken to mean that the states can do as they please.

The challengers nevertheless have identified what they believe are two hooks in the Constitution on which they hope to hang an implied prohibition of the state initiatives that discourage or limit incumbency. One of those points of attack is the Fourteenth Amendment. The other is article I, which in the course of setting up Congress lists a few circumstances that disqualify individuals from congressional office. The Fourteenth Amendment claim is an issue of individual rights—those of voters or candidates. The article I theory, by contrast, is an issue of federalism and the structure of the Constitution.

The arguments that term limitations violate the Constitution have two things in common: First, they ask that state laws be held unconstitutional in the absence of any clear language or principle in the Constitution that requires it. Second, they are incorrect.

State Legislative Power

Structurally, the Constitution superimposed on a group of sovereign states a federal government of limited powers, supreme only when exercising them. It also withdrew a few powers the states had enjoyed, like printing money, but not many.[4] To secure ratification of the controversial document, amendments soon were added listing individual rights protected from federal interference. Those included the Tenth Amendment, which specified that powers not granted to the federal government belonged to the states or the people. A much larger but ill-defined portion of state power was removed after the Civil War by the Fourteenth Amendment. Other amendments followed, many of them designed to alter the election process; amendments were required because the original Constitution had left qualifications for voting in federal elections very much in the control of the states.[5]

---

[3]Declaration of Thomas Foley, Nov. 10, 1993, filed in *Thorsted v. Gregoire*, 841 F.Supp. 1068 (1994).

[4]See art. I, sec. 10.

[5]See the Fifteenth Amendment (voting not abridged based on race); the Seventeenth Amendment (direct election of senators); the Nineteenth Amendment (women's suf-

States of course may not pass laws that interfere with those enacted by Congress, because the Constitution makes the federal laws it authorizes supreme.[6] Nor may states legislate in the face of express prohibitions of the Constitution, many of which are in the Bill of Rights provisions that over the years have been read into the Fourteenth Amendment.

Otherwise, however, the Constitution structurally limits state lawmaking far less than it limits the U.S. Congress. The federal government was created as one of limited, not plenary, powers. Congress can legislate only if given the power to do so in the Constitution. The Roosevelt Court interpreted those powers so broadly that limitations on Congress are scarcely noticed anymore.[7] But the states have never given up their residual plenary power to pass laws. They can legislate as they choose, and by the procedures they choose, unless the federal Constitution, their own constitutions, or Congress prevents them. That truism was even confirmed in the Tenth Amendment—which has not turned out to be much of a restraint on federal power, but whose recognition that any powers not granted to the federal government are retained by the states or the people is unambiguous.[8]

So when the Constitution does not contain any express or implied prohibition of a particular kind of state law, and Congress has done nothing about it, challengers of state legislation must resort to more desperate arguments. Thus it is with term limits.

Ballot Regulations Are Not Term Limitations

Nearly half the states—seventeen so far[9]—have enacted what are popularly called "term-limits" laws. That convenient, but loose,

---

frage); the Twenty-Fourth Amendment (prohibiting poll tax in federal elections); and the Twenty-Sixth Amendment (voting for eighteen-year-olds).

[6]Art. VI, cl. 2.

[7]See, e.g., *Wickard v. Filburn*, 317 U.S. 111 (1942); see also *Heart of Atlanta Motel v. United States*, 379 U.S. 241 (1964).

[8]The Tenth Amendment provides: "The powers not delegated to the United States by the Constitution, nor prohibited by it to the States, are reserved to the States respectively, or to the people."

[9]Arizona, Arkansas, California, Colorado, Florida, Maine, Michigan, Missouri, Montana, Nebraska, North Dakota, Ohio, Oklahoma, Oregon, South Dakota, Washington, and Wyoming.

designation is used here as well. Fifteen of the state laws[10] apply to federal as well as state elections.

However, all but four[11] do not actually limit terms at all, nor restrict anyone from holding office. Most of the initiatives—like the one in Washington of which the Speaker of the House complained—simply provide that after serving some number of terms, an incumbent cannot ask to have his name printed on the ballot and must run as a write-in candidate.

A ballot-access law does not amount to a qualification for holding office; one federal court of appeals reiterated this not long ago.[12] No doubt it is more difficult to win an election without one's name printed on the ballot; that, of course, is the very purpose of such legislation. The goal, as the Supreme Court of California observed when it upheld an absolute bar to reelection of state officers, is a legitimate and rational one: to remove some advantages of incumbents in the interest of "protecting against an entrenched dynastic legislative bureaucracy, and . . . encouraging new candidates to seek public office."[13]

Past congressional elections show, in fact, that winning by write-in certainly is not impossible, particularly for anyone carrying the name-recognition and wielding the other advantages of incumbency. The Supreme Court has held in several cases involving minor-party candidacies that the write-in option is a perfectly adequate alternative for persons not meeting the state's requirements for the ballot.[14] The Supreme Court even held a year ago that there is no constitutional right to run for office at all, in the absence of some sort of "invidious" discrimination.[15]

Reading Words That Aren't There

Consider, however, a law that does not merely restrict ballot access, but actually prohibits serving more than a specified number

[10]All except Maine and Oklahoma.

[11]The exceptions are Colorado, Michigan, Ohio, and Oregon.

[12]*Hopfmann v. Connolly*, 746 F.2d 97, 103 (1st Cir. 1984), *vacated in part on other grounds*, 471 U.S. 459 (1985), *holding reaffirmed on remand*, 769 F.2d 24, 25 n.1 (1st Cir. 1985), *cert. denied*, 479 U.S. 1023 (1987).

[13]*Legislature v. Eu*, 54 Cal. 3d 492, 520, 816 P.2d 1309, 1326 (1991), *cert. denied*, 112 S. Ct. 1292 (1992).

[14]*Munro v. Socialist Workers Party*, 479 U.S. 189 (1986); *American Party v. White*, 415 U.S. 767 (1974); *Storer v. Brown*, 415 U.S. 724 (1974); *Jenness v. Fortson*, 403 U.S. 431 (1971).

[15]*Burdick v. Takushi*, 112 S. Ct. 2059 (1992).

of terms. It is true that the Framers did not enact term limits nation-wide as a matter of federal law by requiring them in the Constitution. No one disagrees with that proposition. But that is not the issue. The legal issue when article I is invoked is whether they went farther and forbade the states to enact any other qualifications—which might include, for example, term limits. There is no evidence that the Framers adopted any such prohibition.

Opponents of term limits like to call the three disqualifications of article I, sections 2 and 3, "the qualifications clauses." The phrase suggests something that is not there. In reality, of course, those clauses do not list qualifications—much less *the* qualifications. They are worded entirely in the negative. They list some disqualifications. They say that "no person shall be" eligible to serve unless of at least a certain age, residency, and duration of citizenship.[16]

The three disqualifications in those clauses of article I are not even the only ones in the Constitution. Several other provisions scattered throughout the Constitution set other disqualifications. No one, for example, may serve in Congress while "holding any Office under the United States."[17] No one may serve in Congress unless he swears or affirms to support the Constitution.[18] A person who is convicted by impeachment may be barred from all federal office.[19] And the Framers contemplated the possibility of still other qualifications or disqualifications as well, because they inserted a clause that "no religious Test shall ever be required as a Qualification" for federal office.[20] Congress over the years has enacted several laws that have disqualified certain categories of persons from holding that office.[21]

---

[16]Art. I, sec. 2, cl. 2 provides: "No person shall be a Representative who shall not have attained to the Age of twenty-five Years, and been seven Years a Citizen of the United States, and who shall not, when elected, be an Inhabitant of that State in which he shall be chosen."

Article I, sec. 3, cl. 3 provides: "No person shall be a Senator who shall not have attained to the Age of thirty Years, and been nine Years a Citizen of the United States, and who shall not, when elected, be an Inhabitant of that State for which he shall be chosen." Senators became subject to election by the people on the adoption of the Seventeenth Amendment in 1913.

[17]Art. I, sec. 6, cl. 2. This was grouped by the authors of the *Federalist* with the other disqualifications of article I. See C. Rossiter, ed., the *Federalist*, no. 52 (New York: New American Library, 1961), p. 325.

[18]Art. VI, cl. 3.

[19]Art. I, sec. 3, cl. 7.

[20]Art. VI, cl. 3.

[21]See Test Oath, Act of July 2, 1868, cl. 128, 12 Stat. 502 (requiring oath not to have supported enemies of the United States); 5 U.S.C. 7313 (disqualifying for five years

It would be odd to suppose that a provision listing some categories of ineligibility, as article I does, somehow should mean that there can be no others, even if enacted by the people of the states. Yet that is the assertion on which most of the legal attacks on state term-limits laws depend. The claim is that the three listed disqualifications are somehow intended to preclude state laws that set additional qualifications.

But no one said such a thing at the Constitutional Convention. No one said so in the ratification debates. That argument seems to have originated a generation later, springing full-blown from the brow of Joseph Story for his treatise in 1833, with no other authority to support it, and contrary to earlier views. Story said his objection to state qualification laws, which he acknowledged existed, was based on "fair reasoning" because he thought such state power dangerous.[22] His formula since has been repeated from time to time, without any better reasoning, by some lower courts. But the Supreme Court has never had to decide the point, and there are many reasons why it should not want to take such a leap, unsupported in text or history.

Moreover, the record of the Constitutional Convention shows that Edmund Randolph's original draft note in the Committee of Detail, which first prepared article I, had read:

> 5. The qualifications of (a) delegates shall be the age of twenty five years at least, and citizenship: (*and any person possessing these qualifications may be elected* except).[23]

---

persons convicted of riot or civil disorder); 5 U.S.C. 7311 (disqualifying permanently persons who strike against the government or advocate its overthrow). Such laws were enacted by the very first Congress. See Act of April 30, 1790, ch. 9, sec. 21, 1 Stat. 112, 117; some such laws have applied only to members of Congress. See Act of July 16, 1862, ch. 180, 12 Stat. 577 (taking money for procuring contracts); Act of June 11, 1864, ch. 119, 13 Stat. 123 (accepting compensation in matter where United States is a party). See generally *DeVeau v. Braisted*, 363 U.S. 144, 159 (1960) (opinion announcing judgment).

[22]Joseph Story, *Commentaries on the Constitution* of the United States (Boston: Hilliard, Gray and Co., 1833), pp. 99–101, sections 623–24. Jefferson, on the other hand, had said that the disqualifications in article I did not "prohibit to the State the power of declaring . . . any other disqualifications which its particular circumstances may call for." Ford, ed., *The Works of Thomas Jefferson* (New York: G. P. Putnam's Sons, 1905), vol. II, p. 380.

[23]Farrand, p. 139.

But the emphasized language—which would indeed have made the listed qualifications exclusive—was eliminated by the committee when it made its report to the convention.[24] Thus the committee that drafted article I considered—and rejected—the very provision that challengers of term limits would pretend is there.

When Madison and Hamilton spoke of qualifications as being "fixed," they were speaking of congressional power, not state. Thus at the convention, Madison, in opposing a provision to empower *Congress* to set property qualifications, said:

> The qualifications *of electors and elected* were fundamental articles in a Republican Govt. and ought to be fixed by the Constitution. If the [federal] Legislature could regulate those of either, it can by degrees subvert the Constitution.[25]

And in the *Federalist,* no. 60, Hamilton similarly wrote that

> The truth is that there is no method of securing to the rich the preference apprehended but by prescribing qualifications of property either for those who may elect or be elected. But this forms no part of the power to be conferred *upon the national government.* Its authority would be expressly restricted to the regulation of the *times,* the *places,* and the *manner* of elections. The qualifications of *the persons who may choose or be chosen,* as has been remarked upon other occasions, are defined and fixed in the Constitution, and are unalterable by the [federal] legislature.[26]

Those statements make plain that they were discussing the powers to be granted or denied to *Congress,* not to the states. What the Framers worried about was the conflict of interest if members of Congress were allowed to set their own qualifications.

Just as importantly, when Madison and Hamilton referred to qualifications being "fixed" by the Constitution, they referred at the same time to *voters* (electors) as well as to members of Congress: "qualifications of electors and elected" in Madison's words, "qualifications of the persons who may choose or be chosen" in Hamilton's. But there was never any doubt that the Constitution leaves the qualifications of *voters* entirely up to each state (as long as they are

---

[24]Ibid., p. 137, n. 6, p. 178.

[25]Ibid., pp. 249–50 (emphasis supplied).

[26]The *Federalist,* no. 60, p. 371 (first and final emphases supplied).

the same as those the state set for voters for the lower house of the state legislature).[27] Those qualifications were fixed by the Constitution only in the sense that *Congress* could not change them; the states were left free to do so, and frequently did. So "fixed," as used by Madison and Hamilton, could not possibly have meant beyond the power of the state legislatures: otherwise the quoted statements, because they referred to voters as well as representatives, would have made no sense. Madison in fact assured that

> The election of the President and Senate will depend, in all cases, on the legislatures of the several States. And the election of the House of Representatives will equally depend on the same authority in the first instance; and will, probably, forever be conducted by the officers and according to the laws of the States.[28]

Moreover, the power of the states to regulate federal elections was confirmed in article I, section 4.

Confusing State Power with Congressional Power

The authors of the Constitution did discuss the possibility of added qualifications for congressional office. They did so entirely out of worry that *Congress* might enact some, and they did not like that idea at all. The records of the debates show great mistrust by the Framers that congressional incumbents, if given the opportunity, might enact qualifications for office designed to lock themselves into power. The delegates worried that if congressional incumbents could add qualifications, then if Congress were "composed of any particular description of men, of lawyers for example . . . the future elections might be secured to their own body."[29]

Although article I, section 4, allows Congress power to override state regulation of elections for Congress, that power seems to have been intended only to deal with state laws that threatened the existence of the federal government itself; the example Alexander Hamilton gave was, what if the states tried to shut down the House by

[27]Art. I, sec. 2, cl. 1, which provides: "The House of Representatives shall be composed of Members chosen every Second Year by the People of the several States, and the Electors in each State shall have the Qualifications requisite for Electors of the most numerous Branch of the State Legislature."

[28]The *Federalist*, no. 44, p. 287.

[29]Farrand, p. 250 (Hugh Williamson of North Carolina).

refusing to hold elections at all? Apart from such extremities, however, he assured that the authors of the Constitution "have submitted the regulation of elections for the federal government, in the first instance, to the local administrations."[30]

With the records that exist, one could certainly craft a respectable argument that the Framers—who tried to list with specificity what powers Congress would have—did not intend to let the congressmen themselves decide qualifications for being a congressman.

The states, however, are a different story. The constitutional debates contain not one word about restricting state powers over federal elections, other than whatever might be enacted through exercise of the congressional override power noted above. And article I, section 4, even reiterated state power to regulate the "Times, Places and Manner" of elections for Congress.[31]

Initiatives, in fact, like the ones used to enact term limits, are acts of "the People," who are assigned by article I and the Seventeenth Amendment to choose representatives and senators. As the Supreme Court of California observed, "It would be anomalous to hold that a statewide initiative measure . . . is invalid as an unwarranted infringement of the rights to vote and seek public office."[32] And the Supreme Court of the United States has explained that article I, section 4, grants power that is very broad. Under it, "The States are given . . . a wide discretion in the formulation of a system for the choice by the people of representatives in Congress."[33] The Supreme Court has recognized that:

> the States have evolved comprehensive, and in many respects complex, election codes regulating in most substantial ways, with respect to both *federal* and state elections, the time, place, and manner of holding primary and general elections, the registration and qualifications of voters, and the selection *and qualification of candidates.*[34]

---

[30]The *Federalist*, no. 59, pp. 362–63.

[31]Art. I, sec. 4, cl. 1, which provides: "The Times, Places and Manner of holding Elections for Senators and Representatives, shall be prescribed in each State by the Legislature thereof; but the Congress may at any time by Law make or alter such Regulations, except as to the Places of chusing Senators."

[32]*Legislature v. Eu*, 54 Cal. 3d 492, 525, 816 P.2d 1309, 1329 (1991).

[33]*United States v. Classic*, 313 U.S. 299, 311 (1941).

[34]*Storer v. Brown*, 415 U.S. 714, 730 (emphasis supplied).

"It cannot be doubted that these comprehensive words [of article I, section 4] embrace authority to provide a complete code for congressional elections . . . ."[35]

Past Practice

All that was confirmed by the actions of the states as soon as the Constitution was ratified. Virginia immediately adopted a law requiring that representatives in Congress be landed property owners (freeholders) and residents not just of the state, but of their respective districts.[36] Georgia and North Carolina also required district residency for various periods.[37] So did Maryland and Massachusetts.[38] New Jersey set up a preliminary nominating process, and limited election to one of the persons so nominated.[39] New states also felt free to add qualifications: Tennessee in 1796 required state residency for three years.[40]

There is no doubt that some writers and some lower courts, from time to time, in one context or another, have said that they thought added qualifications for federal office would be unconstitutional. Most relied on the argument of Justice Joseph Story, some on misreading of the Supreme Court decision in *Powell v. McCormack*, discussed below. But until recently, there have been no state term-limits laws or ballot-access restrictions dealing with incumbency to consider.

At the same time, state and even federal laws have been enacted that prohibit certain persons from holding federal office,[41] and a state law forbidding judges from doing so was upheld by the Supreme Court not long ago.[42] For restrictions on state officeholding, there has been a clean sweep upholding such laws. For those directed to representatives and members of Congress, the results are still

---

[35]*Roudebush v. Hartke*, 405 U.S. 15, 24 (1972), quoting *Smiley v. Holm*, 285 U.S. 355, 366 (1932).

[36]Va. Act of Nov. 20, 1788, ch. 2, sec. II; see also, Va. Act of Dec. 26, 1792, ch. 1, sec. II.

[37]Ga. Act of Jan. 23, 1789, p. 247; N.C. Act of Dec. 16, 1789, ch. 1, sec. I.

[38]Md. Act of Dec. 22, 1788, ch. 10, sec. VII; Mass. Res. of Nov. 20, 1788, ch. 49.

[39]N.J. Act of Nov. 21, 1788, ch. 241, sec. 3.

[40]Tenn. Act of Aug. 3, 1796, ch. 1, sec. 2.

[41]See note 21.

[42]*Clements v. Fashing*, 457 U.S. 957 (1982).

in the lower courts and are mixed. A Nebraska court rejected the constitutional challenges.[43] An Arkansas court, resting its decision on state law, added that it would reject a Fourteenth Amendment challenge but that article I barred the restrictions. Both cases are on appeal.[44] A federal court in Florida threw out one challenge as lacking a plaintiff able to show injury.[45] Suits are pending in trial courts in Florida and Washington.[46] It is quite uncertain, however, how far the federal cases will proceed, and whether the state decisions will be heard by the Supreme Court, because nearly all the recent term-limits laws will not affect any incumbents until nearly the year 2000 or even afterward. Courts, particularly federal courts, do not readily jump into the future to rule on situations that have not arisen or disputes lying three elections in the future.

Misreading Powell v. McCormack

The Supreme Court case most often cited by term-limits opponents is the 1969 decision, written by Chief Justice Earl Warren, in which Representative Adam Clayton Powell challenged the refusal of the

[43]*Duggan v. Beerman*, No. 485, p. 277 (Dist. Ct., Lancaster Co., Sept. 28, 1992), *appeal pending*, No. S-92-907 (S. Ct. Neb.).

[44]*Hill v. Tucker*, No. 92-6171 (Cir. Ct., Pulaski Co., July 29, 1993 and Sept. 8, 1993), *appeal pending sub nom. U.S. Term Limits, Inc. v. Hill*, No. 93-1240 (S. Ct. Ark.). In a 3-2 pre-election decision that contained no reasoning, the Supreme Court of Nevada declared that a term-limits initiative would be unconstitutional. *Stumpf v. Lau*, 839 P.2d 120 (Nev. 1992).

[45]*Leonard v. Smith*, No. 92-1060-Civ-J-10 (U.S. Dist. Ct., M.D. Fla., April 16, 1993).

[46]*Plante v. Smith*, No. 92-CV-40410-WS (U.S. Dist. Ct., N.D. Florida); *Thorsted v. Gregoire*, 841 F.Supp. 1068 (1994). In *Thorsted*, the court found a violation of the First and Fourteenth Amendments as well as of article I—a ruling totally at variance with the many cases that have held state term-limits laws do not violate those provisions. The trial judge wrote a lengthy but extremely selective opinion, failing to mention the deletion in 1787 of a provision that would have made the article I qualifications exclusive; the fact that about half the states after ratifying the Constitution passed laws adding qualifications of property ownership, district residency, or compliance with special nomination requirements; and the Supreme Court's explicit rejection of an article I argument in *Storer* v. *Brown*. The Court concluded that write-in candidacy was not good enough; but it failed to resolve the factual dispute in the record, in which expert affidavits attested that a long-term incumbent would have a good chance of reelection, even by write-in. Those omissions in the *Thorsted* opinion leave the most critical questions ignored instead of answered. Presumably they will be addressed in the pending appeal to the Ninth Circuit, unless the Supreme Court settles them sooner.

House of Representatives to seat him.[47] The Supreme Court held that when the House of Representatives sat in its quasi-judicial role as the "Judge" of the qualifications of a member—under a different constitutional provision, article I, section 5[48]—then that House could not "Judge" on the basis of any qualifications not previously listed in the Constitution. The Court noted the reluctance of the Framers to allow a House to entrench itself in power by setting its own qualifications.[49]

From that holding—that a single House of Congress, acting non-legislatively as a Judge, may not look to qualifications other than those specified in the Constitution—it has sometimes been argued that the people of *states* in 1787 somehow lost the power to enact any qualifications for legislators who are to represent them. But that does not follow at all.

Powell v. McCormack had nothing to do with state regulation of elections. In fact, the Supreme Court specifically noted that it was not considering "the more narrow issue of the power of the States."[50] *Powell* did not even have to do with regulation by a law passed by Congress, for all it involved was the quasi-judicial action of a single House. The Supreme Court has held several times that a single House may not exercise power granted by the Constitution to the full Congress.[51] Here, moreover, the single House was acting not legislatively, but rather as a Judge.

Far from supporting those who argue state term limits are unconstitutional, *Powell v. McCormack* actually rejected the argument that even Congress, the focus of the Framers' worry, would lack power to set qualifications. The Court said:

> Petitioners argue that the proceedings manifest the Framers' unequivocal intention to deny either branch of Congress the authority to add to or otherwise vary the membership qualifications expressly set forth in the Constitution. *We do not completely agree, for the debates are subject to other interpretations.*[52]

[47]*Powell v. McCormack*, 395 U.S. 486 (1969).

[48]Art. I, sec. 5, cl. 1, provides: "Each House shall be the Judge of the Elections, Returns, and Qualifications of its own Members...."

[49]*Powell*, p. 535.

[50]Ibid., p. 543.

[51]E.g., *INS v. Chadha*, 462 U.S. 919 (1983).

[52]*Powell*, p. 532 (emphasis supplied). The Court went on to hold that such a conclusion was acceptable only "in the context of the ... distinction the Framers made

And in a decision a few years later, the Supreme Court explained that *Powell* had involved only "the power of each House to judge." It added that Congress was not necessarily precluded from enacting qualifications, pointing out that "whatever power Congress may have to legislate" was granted in article I, section 4.[53]

Fourteenth Amendment

Another argument advanced against term limits invokes the constitutional provision that has been the nemesis of many state laws: the Fourteenth Amendment, with its general language about due process, equal protection, and all the Bill of Rights restrictions that the Supreme Court has read into it.

Applied to term limits, however, the Fourteenth Amendment is not much of an obstacle. For if term limitations unduly restrict rights of association, or somehow deny equal protection of the laws (although they subject all citizens to the same rules), then it is not just limits on members of Congress that go out the window. The same reasoning would invalidate the limits on state officeholding that many states have included in their constitutions for many years. More than half the states, for example, limit the terms of their governors.[54] Such restrictions have been upheld in countless court decisions, as recently as the decision of the highest court of New York in October 1993 that allowed the voters of New York City last month to limit terms of officeholders in the city government.[55]

Arguments that Fourteenth Amendment rights of association are violated also fly in the face of many other familiar laws and much precedent. Elections are one of the most heavily regulated industries in the United States. Since the states began holding primaries, there have been laws allowing some names on the ballot and keeping others off, and the Supreme Court has allowed them all unless they were being used to protect incumbents from challengers or to close out the poor or members of particular unpopular groups. The Supreme Court has held that there is no constitutional right to run

---

between the power to expel and the power to exclude," i.e., only as a construction of art. I, sec. 5.

[53]*Buckley v. Valeo,* 421 U.S. 1, 133 (1976).

[54]See *Miyazawa v. City of Cincinnati,* 825 F.Supp. 816, 821 (S.D. Ohio 1993).

[55]*Roth v. Cuevas,* 82 N.Y.2d 791 (1993), *affirming* 158 Misc. 2d 238 (1993).

for office, or to vote for a particular candidate.[56] It tests such legislation simply according to whether it has a rational basis.[57] By that test, term-limits laws certainly pass.

In fact, over the years literally millions of persons have been precluded from seeking federal office by the Hatch Act and state-enacted "little Hatch Acts," which the Supreme Court has always upheld.[58] Courts have even allowed such disqualifications to be extended to private individuals closely associated with government programs.[59] The Fourteenth Amendment, in any of its permutations—free speech, freedom of association, equal protection, due process—based on many court decisions, is an unlikely explosive for a constitutional demolition of term-limits laws.

Applying the Constitution

Does that all mean that the new term-limits laws will coast easily through the courts? Not much that involves litigation is easy or certain. And unhappiness with state enactments can distort constitutional law in two ways.

For the past forty years or so, the dominant complaint among citizens who like government was that Congress and state legislatures would not legislate enough. There was neglect, they thought, of purposes widely believed to be desirable—such as civil rights, or equalizing election districts, or reforming police procedures. And so the notion grew that the awkward necessity of passing a law could be skipped, because if a policy is very, very good, then it must be part of the Constitution—even if the words might be a bit difficult to locate, and when identified might seem a trifle imprecise. The Supreme Court in the Warren era and even after did not discourage that view. The law schools, which once scoffed, came to embrace it as "creative."

This might be called the looking-glass approach to constitutional interpretation: that reading the Constitution is like looking in a mirror. One sees reflected the viewpoint one puts before it.

[56]*Burdick v. Takushi; Rodriguez v. Popular Democratic Party*, 457 U.S. 1, 9 (1982).

[57]*Burdick v. Takushi; Anderson v. Celebrezze*, 460 U.S. 780, 788 (1983); *Clements v. Fashing*, 457 U.S. 957, 963 (1982).

[58]*United States Civil Service Commission v. National Association of Letter Carriers*, 413 U.S. 548 (1973); *United Pub. Workers v. Mitchell*, 330 U.S. 75 (1947); *Broadrick v. Oklahoma*, 413 U.S. 601 (1973).

[59]*Smith v. Ehrlich*, 430 F.Supp. 818 (D.D.C. 1976).

But just as it would be disconcerting to gaze and find that the highest law lacked some element necessary for social perfection, it also can be unpalatable to suppose that the Constitution permits legislation that seems hasty or disruptive or, if you will, ugly. For anyone who can believe that the Constitution commands whatever he knows is very wise, it is not much of a step to conclude that the same Constitution—somewhere, somehow—also forbids laws he believes very misguided.

Knocking out distasteful state laws, in fact, was the dominant activity of constitutional litigation a 100 years ago. The Supreme Court in those days examined the Constitution only to discover, for example, that when the Fourteenth Amendment was adopted after the Civil War, its authors presciently forbade state laws setting maximum hours of work.[60] More recently, as pesky state majorities have passed laws that passionate minorities have found objectionable, the losers again have turned to the courts and urged that something in the Constitution forbids such folly. The Court has sometimes obliged, discovering for example a wide-ranging but atextual "right of privacy,"[61] and lately even removing the stake that for a few years had impaled the once-loathsome phrase "substantive due process"[62]—the notion that courts, guided by nothing in the Constitution but the words "due process," may second-guess legislative decisions about the substance of laws.

It is such an approach to constitutional decisionmaking—not the approach of judicial modesty and restraint, but one the Supreme Court has sporadically fallen into—that is the greatest threat to term-limits laws. If the courts feel free to rule as they please, if the Constitution's words and history are no constraint, then law becomes what Justice Jackson called a "crazy zig-zag line between validity and invalidity which can be drawn by a Court which has taken to 'finding' its social judgments in the Constitution."[63] If, on the other hand, state term-limits laws are judged by the constitutional tests of text, history, and precedent, then they easily should pass muster.

[60]E.g., *Lochner v. New York,* 198 U.S. 45 (1905); *Morehead v. New York ex rel. Tipaldo,* 298 U.S. 587 (1936).

[61]E.g., *Roe v. Wade,* 410 U.S. 113 (1973).

[62]E.g., *Reno v. Flores,* 113 S. Ct. 1439, 1447 (1993); *Zinermon v. Burch,* 494 U.S. 113, 125 (1990); but compare, e.g., *Ferguson v. Skrupa,* 372 U.S. 726 (1963).

[63]R. Jackson, *The Struggle for Judicial Supremacy* (New York: Alfred A. Knopf, 1941), p. 66.

Conclusion

Justice Holmes pointed out that what we call law amounts to a prophecy of what the judges will do.[64] His contemporary Sigmund Freud had some insights, too, having to do with the ease of believing what one wants. Praise of the policy advantages of frequent turnover may not always deeply move federal judges, appointed for life with the support of their senators.

Some people may experience—at least until they think about it— a sort of gut feeling that it is unheard of for states to regulate incumbency in Congress. But it is unheard of—i.e., new—because it has not until lately been necessary. Being unfamiliar does not make it unconstitutional—particularly when it seeks the very ends the Framers of the Constitution thought that by frequent elections they had already achieved.[65]

The best that lawyers can do in predicting is to look at the sources judges are supposed to consult—constitutional text; constitutional history; precedent; purpose and basis for the law—and see where these lead. If that is the constitutional analysis applied to term-limits laws, then some tenancies in the House and Senate office buildings may soon be turning over.

[64]Holmes, "The Path of the Law," *Harvard Law Review* 10 (1897): 457, 461.
[65]See Will, pp. 73–91.

9. Congressional Term Limits and the Constitution

Daniel Hays Lowenstein

Voters in Colorado in 1990, and in fourteen additional states in 1992, approved initiative measures limiting those states' senators to two terms and their representatives to from three to six terms. During that same period, many states and municipalities adopted term limits for state and local legislative bodies. Claims that state and local term limits violate the First Amendment or the equal protection clause are foreseeable, but they are unlikely to succeed.[1] Congressional term limits stand on a different footing, because they violate the qualifications clauses of the Constitution.

The primary qualifications for members of the House of Representatives are specified in article I, section 2, clause 2 of the Constitution:

> No person shall be a Representative who shall not have attained to the Age of twenty-five Years, and been seven Years a Citizen of the United States, and shall not, when elected, be an Inhabitant of that State in which he shall be chosen.

Virtually identical language in article I, section 3, clause 3, establishes qualifications for senators, except that the minimum age is thirty and the period of citizenship is nine years.

A longer paper on this subject, entitled "Are Congressional Term Limits Constitutional?" was presented at the annual meeting of the American Political Science Association in Washington, D.C., on September 3, 1993. A copy of my APSA paper was submitted to the U.S. District Court in *Thorsted v. Gregoire*, 841 F.Supp. 1068 (1994). Since Judge Dwyer's well-crafted opinion in that case was issued just before this article was sent to press, and since that opinion is consistent in every material respect with the analysis of this paper, I shall make no further reference to the *Thorsted* litigation.

[1]Such claims were rejected in *Legislature v. Eu*, 816 P.2d 1309 (1991); *cert. denied* 112 S.Ct. 1292 (1992), *cert. denied* sub nom *Californians for Citizen Government v. Legislature*, 112 S.Ct. 1293 (1992). Term limits may also be challenged under state constitutional provisions. The outcomes will depend on the vagaries of state law. Such local challenges have failed in Arkansas, California, and Maine.

To defend the constitutionality of any of the congressional term limits that have been adopted, proponents must establish at least one of the following three propositions:

- Despite the Constitution's enumeration of certain qualifications for members of Congress, states are permitted to establish additional qualifications.
- Even if the Constitution precludes additional qualifications, term limitations are not qualifications within the meaning of this constitutional ban.
- Even if absolute term limits violate the qualifications clauses, the limits that have been adopted in several states are valid because they are not absolute term limits. Rather, they are what I shall refer to in this paper as "quasi-term limits." Instead of prohibiting an individual who has served the specified number of terms from being elected, they merely prohibit the candidate's name from appearing on the ballot.[2] Quasi-term limits are not qualifications but instead are regulations of the "Times, Places, and Manner" of elections, which states are permitted to enact under article I, section 4, clause 1 of the Constitution, subject to overruling by Congress.

The remainder of this paper will be devoted to explaining why each of these propositions is false. The conclusion follows that congressional term limits are unconstitutional.

The Qualifications for Congress Set Forth in the Constitution Are Exclusive

The Constitution, while it establishes certain qualifications for members of Congress, is silent as to whether additional qualifications may be imposed. The crucial question of interpretation is: are these qualifications minimums, to which others may be added, or are they a complete statement of qualifications, to which either addition or subtraction would require an amendment to the Constitution?

In legal language, as in ordinary English, an enumeration of the sort contained in the qualifications clauses may imply exclusivity,

---

[2]The states that have adopted quasi-term limits are Arizona, Arkansas, California, Florida, Montana, Nebraska, North Dakota, Washington, and Wyoming. The states that have adopted absolute term limits are Colorado, Michigan, Missouri, Ohio, Oregon, and South Dakota.

but this is not always the case. It is worth considering a homely example.

Suppose I am having lunch with my son and each of us knows that there are apples, pears, and ice cream in the kitchen. If I say to my son, "You may have an apple or a pear for dessert,": I may well mean, and my son may well understand, that one or the other fruit is all he may have—that is, that he may not have ice cream. My statement will be interpreted as an exclusive listing of permissible desserts. However, if I say, "You may have some ice cream for dessert," I probably intend no such exclusivity. If my son prefers to eat an apple or a pear, he will be free to do so. Like the Constitution's enumeration of certain qualifications for members of Congress, my statements are ambiguous in the sense that it is impossible to know from their language alone whether an exclusive listing is intended. Their grammatical structures are identical, yet the probable meanings are different. As the example shows, however, the context may make it possible to resolve the grammatical ambiguity with confidence.

The ambiguity created by the qualifications clauses was authoritatively resolved by the Supreme Court in *Powell v. McCormack*.[3] In that case, Adam Clayton Powell had been duly elected and satisfied the age, residency, and citizenship requirements imposed by the Constitution, but was excluded from membership by the House of Representatives for various misdeeds. The Supreme Court ruled in Powell's favor on the ground that the Constitution established the exclusive qualifications for Congress, and that therefore the House could not exclude an elected candidate on any other ground.[4]

Those who claim that the qualifications clauses are not exclusive must either seek to have *Powell* overruled or must seek to distinguish it. The case for overruling *Powell* is a very weak one. The case has been criticized by some on the ground that the Court should not have intervened in a matter entrusted by the Constitution to the House of Representatives. However, the only aspect of *Powell* that is relevant here, the ruling that the qualifications clauses are exclusive, provoked no dissent on the Court and has received little or no criticism by outside commentators.[5] The Court's resolution of the

[3]395 U.S. 486 (1969)

[4]Ibid., pp. 521–22.

[5]Even writers defending the constitutionality of congressional term limits have usually avoided criticism of *Powell*. One exception is Stephen J. Safranek, "Term

textual ambiguity was based on an extensive review of historical evidence that led, on balance, to recognition of "the Framers' understanding that the qualifications for members of Congress had been fixed in the Constitution."[6]

Space does not permit a complete review of the historical evidence, but a couple of examples will show that *Powell* stands on firm ground. On August 10, 1787, the Constitutional Convention in Philadelphia had before it a draft containing congressional qualifications similar to those eventually adopted, but also permitting Congress to establish property qualifications. During the August 10 debate, James Madison argued for the deletion of the section containing this authorization, stating that

> The qualifications of electors and elected were fundamental articles in a Republican Govt. and ought to be fixed by the Constitution.[7]

Not everyone agreed with Madison. Gouverneur Morris moved to *expand* Congress's power by deleting the words "with regard to property," thus permitting qualifications of any sort. Morris's motion was defeated, and later the Convention accepted Madison's position when it deleted the section altogether.

The strenuous debate on these motions proves beyond doubt that the delegates believed they were debating matters of substance and not mere questions of surplus language. If the delegates to the Convention did not assume that the qualifications stated in the Constitution were exclusive, then their defeat of Morris's motion would have been meaningless. The *only* way to give substantive meaning to the August 10 actions of the Convention is to interpret the qualifications clauses as exclusive.

The post-convention debates on ratification confirm that the qualifications clauses were generally understood to be exclusive. Both Madison and Alexander Hamilton expressed this view in *The Federalist Papers*. In the *Federalist*, no. 52, Madison wrote:

Limitations: Do the Winds of Change Blow Unconstitutional?," *Creighton Law Review* 26 (1993): 321. For a detailed rebuttal of the arguments of Safranek and each of the other defenders of term limits cited in this paper, see my longer paper, referred to in the first (unnumbered) note.

[6]*Powell*, p. 540.

[7]Max Farrand, ed., *The Records of the Federal Convention of 1787* (1911; New Haven, Conn.: Yale University Press, 1966), vol. 2, p. 249.

The qualifications of the elected, being less carefully and properly defined by the State constitutions [than the qualifications of electors], and being at the same time more susceptible of uniformity, have been very properly considered and regulated by the convention. . . .Under these reasonable limitations, the door of this part of the federal government is open to merit of every description, whether native or adoptive, whether young or old, and without regard to poverty or wealth, or to any particular profession of religious faith.[8]

Unless it was understood that the qualifications in the Constitution were maximums as well as minimums, Madison's praise of the Convention's regulation of qualifications as keeping the door open would be unjustified. Hamilton was even more explicit in the *Federalist*, no. 60:

The qualifications of the persons who may choose or be chosen. . . are defined and fixed in the Constitution, and are unalterable by the legislature.[9]

Antifederalists would have been strenuously opposed to a discretionary power to add new qualifications for members of the national legislature. The fact that there were almost no Antifederalist attacks on the Constitution on this ground is substantial evidence that the opponents of the Constitution shared the view of supporters such as Madison and Hamilton that the qualifications clauses were exclusive.

It is at best questionable whether even a plausible case could be made that the qualifications clauses were understood by the Framers of the Constitution to be nonexclusive. And if one gives any credence at all to *stare decisis*, a plausible case would be insufficient. *Powell v. McCormack* should not be overruled simply because—by hypothesis—it could plausibly have been decided the other way. To justify overruling such a well-established precedent, it must be shown that the conclusion it reached was not plausible. This cannot be done.

Accordingly, those who would argue that the qualifications clauses are not exclusive must seek to distinguish *Powell* on the ground that it ruled that *Congress* was unable to add qualifications

[8]C. Rossiter, ed., *The Federalist Papers* (New York: New American Library, 1961), p. 326.

[9]Ibid., p. 371.

but did not address the question of whether the *states* could do so.[10] That attempt fails because it is contrary (1) to history, (2) to the massive weight of authority, and (3) to the interpretive logic of *Powell*.

History. When the dangers of allowing the creation of open-ended new qualifications were catalogued during the constitutional debates, the danger of abuse from the national legislature's controlling its own membership was most commonly cited. It does not follow that the Framers intended for the states to be able to add qualifications. To the contrary, it is more likely that the addition of qualifications by states was not discussed because no one regarded it as a serious possibility. In any event, the danger of abuse by the national legislature was a prominent argument, but not the only one. The importance of letting the people freely decide who would be their representatives, as in Madison's the *Federalist*, no. 52, quoted above, was an equally prominent argument. Furthermore, at certain moments in the constitutional debates—particularly in the debates that led to omitting any *durational* period of residence in the state as a qualification—the concern over qualifications was directed at parochial regulations that would have been more likely to originate from the states than from Congress, if additional qualifications had been permitted.

Authority. The specific question of the states' authority to add qualifications to those enumerated in the Constitution was not before the court in *Powell*, but the Supreme Court implied the states had no such power in *Storer v. Brown*.[11] In *Storer*, the Court rejected the contention that a one-year party nonaffiliation rule for independent candidates was void as "an additional requirement for the office of Representative." If states were permitted to add qualifications, it would have been irrelevant whether the nonaffiliation rule was "an additional requirement."

Other courts have been more explicit. In particular, courts of at least 23 states have considered whether the state was empowered to impose its own qualifications on candidates for Congress. Every

---

[10]The leading statement of this view is in Roderick M. Hills, Jr., "A Defense of State Constitutional Limits on Federal Congressional Terms," *University of Pittsburgh Law Review* 53 (1991): 97. See also Robert C. DeCarli, Note, "The Constitutionality of State-Enacted Term Limits Under the Qualifications Clauses," *Texas Law Review* 71 (1993): 865.

[11]415 U.S. 724 (1974), p. 746 n. 16.

one of them answered in the negative. One federal court commented on the "singular unanimity" with which state courts have so held,[12] and the federal courts that have considered the question, though fewer in number, have been equally unanimous.[13] The nonjudicial authority recognizing that the exclusivity of the qualifications clauses extends to the states as well as the national government is equally weighty. James Kent[14] and Joseph Story,[15] the great nineteenth century commentators on the Constitution, whose views that the qualifications clauses were exclusive influenced later interpreters, particularly emphasized the states' lack of power to add qualifications.

Logic. The most fundamental flaw in the effort to limit the implied exclusivity of the qualifications clauses is that it misconceives *Powell*'s logic and the nature of the interpretive issue that *Powell* resolved. As a matter of language, the silence of the qualifications clauses is susceptible to the meaning that the qualifications set forth are exclusive, and it is susceptible to the meaning that the enumerated qualifications are minimums to which additional qualifications may be added. But the nature of the ambiguity leaves no room for an in-between interpretation. To return to my previous example, if both of my sons are present and I say, "There is fruit for dessert," my statement may or may not be interpreted as an exclusive listing, but under no plausible interpretation (barring additional background facts that alter the context) does it mean that one son may have ice cream but the other may not.

It is for this reason that the effort to distinguish *Powell* fails. It is true that in *Powell*, the Court did not have before it the question of whether states could add qualifications. But because the ambiguity in the Constitution is an either/or ambiguity, the Court's determination that Congress has no power to add qualifications resolved that ambiguity once and for all. *Powell* is based on "the Framers' understanding that the qualifications for members of Congress had been fixed in the Constitution."[16] That interpretation of the Constitution—though

---

[12]*Stack v Adams*, 215 F.Supp. 1295 (N.D. Fla. 1970).

[13]For reference to the state and federal decisions referred to in this paragraph, see my paper cited in the first (unnumbered) note.

[14]See James Kent, *Commentaries on American Law*, 3rd ed. (1836), vol. 1, p. 228.

[15]See Joseph Story, *Commentaries on the Constitution of the United States* (Boston: Hilliard, Gray & Co., 1833), vol. 2, pp. 98–103 (sections 622–27).

[16]*Powell*, p. 540.

admittedly not the Court's actual holding in *Powell*, given the particular controversy it had before it—is as conclusive for qualifications added by the states as it is for qualifications added by Congress.

Term Limits Are Qualifications of the Type Proscribed by the Constitution

The fact that I am over thirty years of age, have been a citizen of the United States for more than nine years, and am an inhabitant of California does not, in itself, give me a claim to one of California's seats in the Senate. Plainly, some things other than age, citizenship, and residency keep most of us out of Congress without violating the qualifications clauses. Can term limits be defended on the ground that they do not impose "qualifications" of the sort prohibited by the Constitution?[17] Case law recognizes two types of restrictions that states may impose without violating the principle that the qualifications set forth in the Constitution are exclusive.

Election procedures. One constitutional qualification for service in Congress is so basic that it is not often cited as a qualification at all: one must be elected. The Constitution empowers state legislatures to prescribe the "Times, Places and Manner" of holding congressional elections, subject to control by Congress.[18] Election regulations and procedures may have the effect of eliminating some candidates at various stages. Indeed, that is likely to be their intent, so that at the final stage the voters are provided with a small enough number of candidates that their selection represents a majority, or at a minimum, a substantial plurality preference. Such regulations, so long as they are reasonable and have as their purpose the facilitation rather than the frustration of the voters' ability to choose the representative they prefer, should be regarded as regulations of "Times, Places and Manner" of elections, not as qualifications for office separate from the basic qualification of being elected.

Thus, in *Storer v. Brown*,[19] the Supreme Court upheld a California statute prohibiting independent candidates from appearing on the

---

[17]For efforts to answer this question in the affirmative, see Neil Gorsuch and Michael Guzman, "Will the Gentlemen Please Yield? A Defense of the Constitutionality of State-Imposed Term Limitations," *Hofstra Law Review* 20 (1991): 341; Mark P. Petracca, "A New Defense of State-Imposed Congressional Term Limits," *PS* 26 (December 1993): 700.

[18]Art. I, sec. 4, cl. 1.

[19]415 U.S. 724 (1974).

general election ballot if they had been affiliated with a political party within a year prior to the primary, and therefore, by remaining affiliated with that party, could have sought to appear on the general election ballot by seeking nomination in the primary. The principle recognized in *Storer* does not provide a constitutional defense for term limits. Term limitations are not election procedures and do not simply prescribe a particular course for seeking election for candidates who have run up against the limit. Rather, they prevent the election of such candidates by any means.

Conditions of candidacy. Many states have made a holder of one office (typically, but not always, a judicial office) ineligible to run for other offices until the term of the first office has expired. Such restrictions have invariably been struck down as unconstitutional qualifications when the office for which the would-be candidate wanted to run was either the Senate or the House of Representatives. More moderate requirements—that candidates for a second office take a leave of absence or resign from the office they already hold— have been enforced against persons running for Congress.

It is not necessary here to trace the nuances of the distinction drawn in these cases,[20] for it is plain that the doctrine that permits some "resign to run" statutes to be applied to congressional candidates does not come close to supporting congressional term limits. Term limitation is much more similar to the unconstitutional "length of the term" ban on candidacies than to constitutional resign-to-run conditions. The only way to avoid the length-of-the-term prohibition is not to be elected to office A at time 1 in order to be eligible to run for office B at time 2. Term limits function in precisely the same way, except that office A and office B are the same.

Under resign-to-run statutes, candidates have the ability to run for Congress simply by resigning from their present offices. This is one, but not the only reason such statutes have been upheld. In addition, the statutes promote "the integrity and independence of the judicial branch," and thereby protect the state's "fundamental interests in the structure of [its own] government."[21] Plainly, members of Congress are not within the "essential regulatory authority of the States," as are the state officials affected by resign-to-run

[20]The leading case, *Signorelli v. Evans*, 637 F.2d 853 (1980), contains a very thoughtful discussion.
[21]Ibid., p 861.

statutes.[22] Furthermore, the resign-to-run statutes have been upheld in part because the reviewing courts have been satisfied that their purpose is to guard the state's interest in performance of the duties of the would-be candidate's present office, not the obstruction of that person's desire to be elected to Congress. The opposite is the case for term limits.

Powell v. McCormack defined the scope of the negative implication it found contained in the qualifications clauses:

> The Constitution leaves the House without authority to exclude any person, duly elected by his constituents, *who meets all the requirements for membership expressly prescribed in the Constitution.*[23]

The Constitution sets forth certain requirements a person must satisfy to serve in Congress, the most important of which is being elected. The negative implication that is created by that setting forth of certain requirements extends to all additional requirements. The Supreme Court stated that clearly in *Powell*, and it is hard to see what else could be meant by the proposition that the qualifications clauses are exclusive.

Quasi-Term Limits Fail in Their Attempt to Evade the Qualifications Clauses

"Quasi-term limits," it will be recalled, are regulations that preclude the name of a person who has served a specified number of terms in Congress from appearing on the ballot. Granted that absolute term limitations are unconstitutional for the reasons set forth above, can the constitutional ban be evaded by adoption of quasi-term limits? The answer is no, for three different reasons. Like an absolute term limit, a quasi-term limit is an unconstitutional attempt to add to the exclusive qualifications for Congress set forth in the Constitution. Unlike absolute term limits, quasi-term limits are also unconstitutional because they violate equal protection and First Amendment rights of affected candidates and their supporters, and because they violate the associational rights of political parties to nominate the qualified candidates of their choice.

[22]See *Joyner v. Mofford*, 706 F.2d 1523 (1983), p. 1530.

[23]*Powell*, p. 522 (emphasis added, emphasis in original deleted).

The Qualifications Clauses. The most appropriate basis for striking down quasi-term limits, because it goes to the heart of the issue, is that they violate the qualifications clauses. That is, quasi-term limits should be seen as what they are: gimmicky evasions of the Constitution. The Court in *Powell* regarded the interpretation of the qualifications clauses as a matter not of dusty history but of great consequence to a democratic society.

> Had the intent of the Framers emerged from these materials with less clarity, we would nevertheless have been compelled to resolve any ambiguity in favor of a narrow construction of the scope of Congress' power to exclude members-elect. A fundamental principle of our representative democracy is, in Hamilton's words, 'that the people should choose whom they please to govern them.' . . . As Madison pointed out at the Convention, this principle is undermined as much by limiting whom the people can select as by limiting the franchise itself.[24]

It is certainly true that many people today believe earnestly that the adoption of term limits will enhance rather than detract from the democratic character of our government. But the Constitution contains procedures for its own amendment precisely because the Framers recognized that beliefs on such matters will change with time.

Supporters of term limits may believe it is too difficult to amend the Constitution when the incumbents in Congress have such an obvious personal stake in resisting term limits. But difficulty is not the same as impossibility. Term-limits supporters can seek to elect new representatives who are pledged to support term limits, or they can seek to persuade state legislatures to call for a constitutional convention. The task facing term-limits proponents does not look especially formidable compared, say, with the one that faced the women who met in Seneca Falls in 1848 and resolved that women should have the right to vote. They waited three-quarters of a century for the Nineteenth Amendment, despite the fact—as even the most passionate believer in term limits must concede—that the justice of their cause was no less compelling than the need for term limits. The undeniable groundswell of opinion in favor of term limits is no reason to allow gimmicks to replace the constitutional-amendment processes. To the contrary, that groundswell should remind us that

[24]Ibid., p. 547.

the difficulty of the amendment process was devised in order to assure that the constitutional structure should not be drastically altered, perhaps for the worse, unless a change in public opinion demonstrates its durability as well as its force.

Aside from these general considerations, which are the most important, there is solid authority that the prohibition on additional congressional qualifications cannot be evaded by denying access to the ballot rather than absolute eligibility for the office. Many cases have struck down state-created qualifications as the basis for excluding candidates from primaries, whose purpose is not the election of a member of Congress but a determination of who will appear on the general election ballot. For example, in a 1946 case (whose interest is heightened by the fact that the beneficiary was an eventually successful Republican candidate for the Senate named Joseph R. McCarthy) the Wisconsin Supreme Court wrote:

> If Mr. McCarthy under Wisconsin law cannot be a candidate for nomination at the primary, he can never be a candidate at the election of any political party. He is therefore disqualified to take the first step if the argument of the relator is sound. His right to be a candidate at the election would be a barren right. Neither by constitutional provision nor legislative enactment can the state of Wisconsin prescribe qualifications of a candidate for *nomination* for the office of United States Senator in addition to those prescribed by the Constitution of the United States.[25]

Courts have struck down state-created qualifications at the nomination stage because barring a candidate from the ballot is tantamount to disqualifying the candidate. As the Wisconsin court wrote, judges thereby assure that the right to run for Congress, subject only to the minimal qualifications in the Constitution, will not be "a barren right."[26]

Equal Protection and the First Amendment. If absolute term limitation does not violate the equal protection clause or the First Amendment, it may be asked, how could quasi-term limits, which are less restrictive, even if only slightly so, be unconstitutional? This question has a straightforward answer. Whatever may be the state's interests in

[25]*State ex rel. Wettengel v. Zimmerman*, 24 N.W.2d 504 (1946), pp. 508–9 (emphasis added).

[26]Ibid., p. 508.

limiting the period of eligibility for public office, it is much more difficult for the state to justify imposing a grave handicap on a candidate who is conceded to be eligible.

Since the 1968 decision in *Williams v. Rhodes*,[27] the denial of a position on the ballot to an eligible candidate has been subject to challenge on equal protection and First Amendment grounds. It is not necessary to trace the intricacies of the doctrine the Supreme Court has developed, for it may be conceded that, for various reasons, the denial of a ballot position on grounds of length of incumbency does not result in an especially strong burden of justification. Nevertheless, on any account, the state must provide some reasonable justification if its restriction is to survive scrutiny.

No matter how misguided some of us may believe absolute term limits are, they are not "irrational" in the sense in which that term is used in constitutional law. In contrast, the exclusion from the ballot of a candidate who is conceded to be qualified, on the ground that in the past the candidate has demonstrated sufficiently strong support in the electorate to be elected and reelected to Congress a specified number of times, runs directly counter to the interests the Court has identified as justifying the exclusion of some candidates from the ballot.

This can be seen most clearly by considering what is by now our old friend, *Storer v. Brown*, which upheld a statute prohibiting a person from running as an independent candidate in the general election if the candidate was registered as affiliated with a political party within a year prior to the primary election. Justice White, speaking for the Court, explained the policy of the statute.

> The direct party primary in California is not merely an exercise or warm-up for the general election but an integral part of the entire election process, the initial stage in a two-stage process by which the people choose their public officers. It functions to winnow out and finally reject all but the chosen candidates. The State's general policy is to have contending forces within the party employ the primary campaign and primary election to finally settle their differences. The general election ballot is reserved for major struggles; it is not a forum for continuing intraparty feuds. The provision against defeated primary candidates running as independents effectuates this aim, the visible result being to prevent the losers

[27]393 U.S. 23 (1968).

from continuing the struggle and to limit the names on the ballot to those who have won the primaries and those independents who have properly qualified. The people, it is hoped, are presented with understandable choices and the winner in the general election with sufficient support to govern effectively.[28]

If quasi-term limits are to be taken seriously as anything other than forbidden qualifications in disguise, then they contemplate that on a regular basis, incumbents over the limit will run as write-in candidates against the winner of the primary in their own party as well as against the nominee of the opposing party. Nothing more sharply in contrast to the orderly process Justice White described in *Storer* could be imagined.

Of course, the states are not constitutionally required to follow the policies Justice White described as justifying the nonaffiliation rule. On the other hand, the election process is so central to democratic government that it is doubtful whether an exclusion of qualified candidates from the ballot can be justified by any state interest not related to facilitating the electorate's opportunity to select the candidate of its choice. No such interest can credibly be put forth in the case of quasi-term limits.

To be sure, proponents will claim that excluding long-term incumbents from the ballot facilitates the election process by offsetting unfair incumbency advantages and thereby equalizing the chances of all candidates. However, barring incumbents from the ballot would go way beyond any effort to equalize the effects of perquisites and other incumbency benefits that can plausibly be described as unfair. The defense of quasi-term limits as attempts to equalize the opportunities of challengers and incumbents is a sham. The only real purpose of quasi-term limits is to frame a practical ban on candidacies in a manner that the proponents hope will evade the qualifications clauses.

Associational Rights of Parties. The quasi-term limit also interferes unconstitutionally with the associational rights of political parties. It prohibits candidates who are fully qualified for the office they seek and who meet all qualifications for party nominees, such as length of affiliation with the party, from seeking the nomination of

[28]*Storer v. Brown*, p. 735.

their party. Likewise, it prevents the party, by any means whatsoever, from nominating the qualified person who may well be the party's choice.

Such an interference with the associational rights of parties is unconstitutional under the doctrine set forth in *Tashjian v. Republican Party of Connecticut*[29] and *Eu v. San Francisco County Democratic Central Committee*.[30] These cases establish in parties a broad immunity from state regulation of their election-related activity. In *Tashjian*, the Court struck down a statute that prevented the Republican Party from permitting independent voters to participate in certain Republican primaries. In *Eu*, the Court struck down a ban on endorsements by party organizations of candidates in party primaries.

The quasi-term limit is vastly more intrusive into a party's ability to function than were the regulations struck down in *Tashjian* and *Eu*. Parties and their voters are barred from considering qualified candidates in their own primaries. By definition, the candidates they are not allowed to nominate are the ones the parties and voters have selected at least twice before. Thus, quasi-term limits typically prohibit voters and parties from nominating the candidates of their choice. Furthermore, if candidates affected by the quasi-term limits pursue the only means of seeking reelection allowed to them, then they and their own parties' nominees are compelled by the state to oppose each other in the general election.

In *Tashjian*, the party's inability to determine which nonmembers could vote in its primaries was less obstructive of associational rights than a party's complete inability to select the nominee of its choice under a quasi-term limit. In *Eu*, the party organization's inability to endorse a candidate who was running in the primary was far less damaging to the party and its ability to function than the inability of the party and its voters to even consider a qualified candidate in the primary.

The only justifications for this heavy-handed party-bashing on the part of the state that can be put forth honestly are themselves constitutionally suspect: (1) a desire to evade the implied restrictions created by the qualifications clauses; and (2) a desire to drastically handicap certain candidates in opposition to the people's right to

[29]479 U.S. 208 (1986).
[30]489 U.S. 214 (1989).

choose the candidate of their choice rather than facilitation of that right. Quasi-term limits are unconstitutional.

Conclusion

Term limitations on congressional candidates impose qualifications in addition to those set forth in the Constitution. As such, they are void under the interpretation of the qualifications clauses that has enjoyed overwhelming judicial and nonjudicial support and that was authoritatively adopted by the Supreme Court in *Powell v. McCormack*. As any constitutional lawyer is likely to agree, interpretive issues as one-sided as this are rare.

The quasi-term limit is a clever attempt to escape the unconstitutionality of absolute term limits, but not clever enough. It cannot evade the ban erected by the qualifications clauses, but its attempt to do so lands it in new, equally fatal constitutional difficulties. In addition, the quasi-term limit denigrates the entire term-limits movement. Whatever the merits of term limits, they are supported by many people who respect the Constitution and wish to strengthen American democracy. The quasi-term limit, which thumbs its nose at the Constitution, should be given short shrift by the courts.

Term limits will soon be taking effect in numerous state legislatures. If the American people perceive that the consequences of term limits are as desirable as their supporters expect, the pressure for congressional term limits will build to the point that a constitutional amendment is inevitable. On the other hand, if term limitation turns out to be more of an impediment to good government than a panacea, mass support will subside before the difficulties of the amendment process can be overcome. Neither scenario presents any reason for bending the Constitution.

10. A Commentary on the Constitutionality of Term Limits

Ronald D. Rotunda

Introduction

During the last several years, the voters in various states have seen fit to use the initiative and the referendum to enact laws that discourage long incumbency on the part of their elected officials. Incumbents can prolong their cling to office through patronage, pork-barrel projects, gerrymandering, name recognition, and voter inertia. Incumbents also have natural advantages in soliciting financial support; thus, if campaign finance laws limit the expenditures of opponents to no more than the expenditures of the incumbents, that also favors sitting legislators.

In recent years, the turnover in the House of Lords has been greater than the turnover in the House of Representatives. There was even more turnover in the membership of the Soviet Politburo. Of the 405 House incumbents who ran in 1990, 20 percent had no major party opponents and 60 percent had opponents who raised less than half the money of the incumbents. Common Cause, the citizen's lobby, says that only 23 House races in 1990 were truly competitive.[1]

The turnover for the Presidency is certainly much greater than the turnover in the House of Representatives. Since the enactment, in 1951, of the Twenty-second Amendment (limiting the President to two terms), only two presidents (Eisenhower and Reagan) have served two full terms. From 1900 to 1951, only Wilson and Franklin D. Roosevelt served two full terms. Many reasons account for this: one is that a House district can be gerrymandered, but the entire country cannot be. Similarly, turnover is greater in the United States Senate than in congressional districts, because one cannot gerrymander a state.

---

[1]Ronald D. Rotunda, "No Impediment to Term Limits," *Washington Post*, February 13, 1993, p. A31.

Many states, as well as the United States itself, place term limits on the chief executive because voters often believe that term limits improve the competition for public office. The evidence supports this belief. For example, after California voted strict term limits for members of the state legislature, over a quarter of the legislature was forced to retire; in the renewed competition for public office, nearly half of the new members were women and more than 20 percent were Hispanic.[2] Consequently, many voters have come to believe that there should be term limits for legislators as well as for governors and Presidents.[3]

The wisdom of term-limits legislation is distinct, however, from the question of constitutionality, and I will focus only on the latter question. Unlike Gaul, this issue is divided into only two main parts. First, does any clause of the Constitution—in particular the qualifications clause—forbid states, or Congress itself, from enacting term-limits legislation; and, second, does Supreme Court case law—in particular, the decision in *Powell v. McCormack*[4]—reject term-limits legislation? If we can illuminate those two issues, we will be able to understand the essence of the constitutional debate.

Does the Constitution Forbid Additions to the Qualifications of Age, Citizenship, and Residency

Many proposals or laws that are called "term-limits laws" do not limit terms or establish qualifications for office at all. Rather, they establish restrictions that limit access to the ballot by long-term incumbents. Voters can still vote for their favorite candidates, but they would have to use the write-in vote.[5] Other proposals limit

[2]"Real Change," *Wall Street Journal*, April 28, 1993, p. A14 (Midwest ed.).

[3]See, e.g., Rotunda; Stephen J. Safranek, *The Constitutional Case for Term Limits: The Courts, the Congress, and the Meaning of Federalism* (Washington, D.C.: U.S. Term Limits Foundation, 1993); Ronald D. Rotunda and John E. Nowak, *Treatise on Constitutional Law: Substance and Procedure* (St. Paul: West Publishing Co., 2d ed. 1992), vol. 1, sec. 9.19 (and latest annual pocket part).

During the last presidential election, in *every* state where a term-limits proposal was on the ballot, more people supported term limits than supported Bill Clinton for President. Kris W. Kobach, "Term Limits and the Seventh and Nineteenth Amendments," *Yale Law Journal* 103 (1994): 1971. Even in Arkansas, while 54 percent of the voters supported their favorite son, 60 percent supported term limits. Ibid.

[4]395 U.S. 486 (1969).

[5]Some of the laws that are called term-limits legislation are more modest than a strict term-limits law. For example, Initiative Measure 573, recently enacted in

consecutive terms. In an effort to level the playing field between the incumbent and challenger, the law would provide that no one could serve more than two or three consecutive terms. The focus of this discussion, however, is on true term-limits legislation, which would prevent anyone from holding a particular office for more than a given number of years. If term-limits legislation is constitutional, then a fortiori, ballot-access legislation, or consecutive term limitations, should pass constitutional muster.

The main constitutional clause at issue is article I, section 2, clause 2, which states that no one may be a representative "who shall not have attained to the Age of twenty-five Years, and been seven Years a Citizen of the United States, and who shall not, when elected, be an Inhabitant of that State in which he shall be chosen." The opponents of term limits typically argue that this language sets forth the *exclusive* qualifications for office, and that there can be no others.[6]

We must realize that to understand article I, section 2, clause 2 to establish *exclusive* qualifications for office would be to apply an atypical method of constitutional interpretation that is hardly compelled by the language of the clause. The Supreme Court does not usually read the Constitution so restrictively. For example, section

Washington state, only limits access to the ballot for long-term incumbents. It prohibits no one from campaigning or serving in office, and voters retain their right to vote for whomever they wish. The Supreme Court has never held that a ballot-access law violated art. I, sec. 2, cl. 2. The Court will uphold ballot-access laws *if* they are reasonable. E.g., *Storer v. Brown*, 415 U.S. 724 (1973).

[6]Opponents of term limits may sometimes refer to other clauses, such as the equal-protection clause of the Fourteenth Amendment or the free-speech (and implied free-associational) right of the First Amendment, and argue that they prevent term limits. However, such an argument proves too much. If the equal protection or free-speech clauses invalidate term limits, that invalidation could not be confined to term limits for legislators only. It would indicate that a term limit on the office of governor would also be unconstitutional. That conclusion would mean that all the state and federal decisions upholding executive branch term limits, written over a time span of many years, would all have to be overturned. Judge Dwyer, in *Thorsted v. Gregoire*, 841 F.Supp. 1068 (1994), actually argued that the Washington state modified term-limits law (actually, a ballot-access law) violated the First and Fourteenth Amendments because it violated "the voters' constitutional freedom of choice" by making certain candidates ineligible "on the basis of incumbency. . . ." That argument proves too much. If a term-limits law violated free speech, then term limits for governors would also violate the First Amendment. It would also mean that the Twenty-second Amendment limiting the President to two terms also amended the First Amendment— a position that no court (or proponent or opponent of the Twenty-second Amendment) has ever advanced before.

2 of the Fourteenth Amendment provides a remedy when a state denies the right to vote to eligible males: that state loses proportionate representation in the House of Representatives. Yet the Supreme Court has held that that remedy is *not* the *exclusive* one: courts can also enforce the right to vote much more effectively by use of the injunction.[7] Although Justice Harlan argued that the enforcement provision of section 2 of the Fourteenth Amendment was the *exclusive* method of enforcing section 1,[8] the majority clearly rejected that method of interpretation.

Similarly, the Twenty-fourth Amendment forbids a poll tax in any election for federal office. However, after that amendment was ratified, the Court held that the earlier enacted Fourteenth Amendment forbids a poll tax in any election, state, or federal.[9] Once again, the Court did not interpret a clause as impliedly creating an *exclusive* list of options.

The Constitution has various provisions and amendments dealing with the death or resignation of the president.[10] None of those has any reference to midterm elections to fill the unexpired term of a President or vice president, although the Constitution does refer to elections to fill the unexpired terms of U.S. Representatives.[11] Yet the 19th century Congress thought that it had the power to enact statutes providing for by-elections for the offices of President and vice president.[12] The opponents of term limits, who often rely on historical understanding in reaching their conclusions, would have to reject the historical evidence that the early Congress thought that it could provide for the election to fill the unexpired term of presidential office, just as many states have a special by-election to fill the remaining term of a representative or senator.

It is more than a little interesting that the qualifications clause, article I, section 2, clause 2, never states that it is establishing *exclusive* qualifications. To argue that the language of this clause nonetheless sets forth the exclusive qualifications for office would be to interpret it in a way that is foreign to the interpretation of other clauses of

---

[7]*Reynolds v. Sims*, 377 U.S. 533 (1964).

[8]Ibid., pp. 503–4 (Harlan, J., dissenting).

[9]*Harper v. Virginia State Board of Elections*, 383 U.S. 663 (1966).

[10]Art. II, sec. 1, cl. 6; Amendments XII, XXI, and XXV.

[11]Art. I, sec. 2, cl. 4.

[12]Revised Statutes of 1874, sections 146–50 (1875).

144

the Constitution. If the Framers meant that qualifications for representatives were exclusively defined by the language of article I, section 2, clause 2, they could easily have said that. After all, when they meant to give the states a limited power to impose duties in order to execute their inspection laws, they said that states could only do so when it was *"absolutely* necessary."[13]

Those who claim that article I, section 2, clause 2 must be read to say that age, U.S. citizenship, and state residency (but not *district* residency, even though federal law, as discussed below, requires representatives to be elected by district) can be the *only* qualifications for office have to deal with the inconvenience that, as so interpreted, that section is inconsistent with other clauses of the Constitution that impose additional qualifications for office. For example, when the Senate impeaches someone, it can impose a disqualification to become a U.S. representative or senator.[14] A cabinet officer is similarly disqualified from being a member of Congress, even though he or she meets the minimum requirements of age, U.S. citizenship, and state residency.[15] Anyone who has taken an oath to support the U.S. Constitution and then engaged in rebellion against the United States is also disqualified from federal office.[16]

When other clauses of the Constitution impose disqualifications, that is equivalent to *adding* to the minimum qualifications of article I, section 2, clause 2. A candidate, besides meeting the qualifications of age, U.S. citizenship, and state residency, must also meet the further qualifications of, for example, not being a cabinet officer. In other words, disqualifications in this context are logically and linguistically equivalent to qualifications. One is the multiplier and the other is the multiplicand.

The way to interpret article I, section 2, clause 2 consistently with the remainder of the Constitution is to conclude that it does not

[13]Art. I, sec. 10, cl. 2 (emphasis added).

[14]Art. I, sec. 3, cl. 7. See also, Rotunda, "Impeaching Federal Judges: Where Are We and Where Are We Going?" *Judicature: The Journal of the American Judicature Society* 72 (1989): 359 (transcript of edited remarks); Rotunda, "An Essay on the Constitutional Parameters of Federal Impeachment," *Kentucky Law Review* 76 (1988): 707; Rotunda, "Impeachment Showdown: Congress versus Judges," *Legal Times,* November 1, 1993, p. 37.

[15]Art. I, sec. 6, cl. 2.

[16]Amendment 14, sec. 3. By a two-thirds vote in each House, Congress may remove this disqualification or disability.

preclude additional, reasonable qualifications that are not otherwise unconstitutional. For example, a law disqualifying Baptists from serving in Congress is otherwise unconstitutional because it would violate the prohibition against religious qualifications found in article VI, clause 3. It would also violate the First Amendment. It is invalid because it violates those other clauses, not because it adds to the qualifications already found in article I. What is crucial, in short, is the nature of the added qualification and not the mere fact that there is an added qualification.

While opponents of term limits often rely on history, the fact of the matter is that the historical understanding of article I, section 2, clause 2 is far from clear. The respected 19th-century commentator, Justice Joseph Story, argued that the qualifications of article I, section 2, clause 2 should be interpreted to be exclusive. In his *Commentaries on the Constitution*, Story asserted that "when the constitution established certain qualifications, as necessary for office, it meant to exclude all others as prerequisites. From the nature of such a provision, the affirmation of these qualifications would seem to imply a negative of all others."[17] The alternative, said Story, would mean that states might provide that "none but a Deist, a Catholic, a Protestant, a Calvinist, or a Universalist, shall be a representative."[18]

Story used this example to support his conclusion that there can be no additional qualifications beyond those of age, citizenship, and state residency, but his reasoning is not persuasive because he was attacking a straw man; he apparently did not appreciate, as discussed above, that the limitations already existing in article VI, clause 3 would prohibit either the state or federal government from imposing any religious qualification for office.

Justice Story admitted that other contemporary commentators did not share his view. He quoted President Jefferson, who concluded that the Constitution did not forbid the states from imposing additional qualifications to the office of senator or representative.[19] Jefferson argued that if it is the rule of interpretation that when the

---

[17]Joseph Story, *Commentaries on the Constitution* (1st ed. 1833), vol. 2, sec. 625, p. 100. It is interesting that in his one-volume abridgment, which Story prepared himself, he left out this section and the argument that it contained. See Ronald D. Rotunda and John E. Nowak, eds., *Joseph Story's Commentaries on the Constitution* (Durham, N.C.: Carolina Academic Press, 1987) (reprint of Joseph Story's own one-volume abridgment of his multivolume treatise, originally published in 1833), p. xxxvii. The one-volume text was very popular in its time and was used as a law school text.

[18]Story, p. 99, sec. 623.

Constitution "assumes a single power out of many," we "should consider it as assuming the whole," then the Constitution "would vest the general government with a mass of powers never contemplated."[20]

Jefferson also referred to the Tenth Amendment, which provides that the powers that the Constitution does not delegate to the federal government "are reserved" to the states. It is interesting that the modern Supreme Court has also relied on the Tenth Amendment in upholding a state constitutional provision requiring state judges to retire at age 70. The plaintiffs objected that the state constitutional provision violated the equal protection clause of the Fourteenth Amendment as well as the Age Discrimination in Employment Act. The Court rejected those claims and held that the authority of the people of the states to determine the qualifications of their "most important government officials" is:

> an authority that lies at "the heart of representative government." It is a power reserved to the States under the Tenth Amendment and guaranteed them by that provision of the Constitution under which the United States "guarantee[s] to every state in this Union a Republican Form of Government."[21]

A term-limitation law, which provides that officials may not hold a particular office for more than a given number of years, is a lot like a mandatory retirement law, which requires certain officials to leave office at age 70. And U.S. senators and representatives are among a state's "most important government officials."

During Story's time, some states began to require that their representatives be elected by district rather than by statewide elections. Also during this period, some states began requiring that elected representatives be residents of the districts that they purported to represent. Story objected to this requirement because it was inconsistent with his argument that states could not add to the article I qualifications of age, U.S. citizenship, and state residency.[22] Yet, as

[19]See Story, p. 100, sec. 624 (referring to and discussing Jefferson's arguments, and quoting *Correspondence of Thomas Jefferson* (London: Henry Colburn and Robert Bentley, 1829), Thomas Jefferson Randolph, ed., vol. 4, pp. 238–39).

[20]Story, p. 100, sec. 624, quoting *Correspondence of Thomas Jefferson*, vol. 4., p. 239.

[21]*Gregory v. Ashcroft*, 111 S.Ct. 2395, 2402 (1991).

[22]Story, p. 100, sec. 624.

he was forced to acknowledge, states were, in fact, imposing such residency qualifications. The historical custom does not support the conclusion that states cannot impose district residency requirements, which are admittedly qualifications that add to those imposed by article I.[23]

While some states imposed district qualifications, other states, during the early part of the 19th century, insisted that their representatives be elected at large. In response, in 1842, Congress enacted a statute *requiring* states to impose a district qualification.[24] Although that statute does not impose a district residency requirement, it still imposes a *district qualification*; that is, it requires that congressmen be elected by district. The district qualification still exists. States are not permitted to have their representatives elected at large. The district requirement is a qualification in addition to the minimum qualifications of age, U.S. citizenship, and state residency, found in the qualifications clause of article I, section 2, clause 2.

For example, assume that a state is divided into ten districts, each composed of two million residents and one million voters. Assume that in district number one, candidate A (of party no. 1) gets 499,000 votes, and loses to candidate B (of party no. 2), who gets 501,000 votes. Let us assume further that no candidate (winner or loser) in any of the other nine districts gets more than 499,000 votes. Perhaps in the other districts, there were third-party candidates, or there was low voter turnout. Even though candidate A received more votes than any other candidate in the state (except for candidate B)—even

[23]There are lower court decisions, using conclusory language, that have invalidated district residency requirements in the few instances where they have been challenged. E.g., *Hellman v. Collier*, 141 A.2d 908 (1958) (per curiam). But see *Williams v. Tucker*, 382 F.Supp. 381, 388 (M.D. Pa. 1974) (per curiam) (rejecting art. I, "Qualifications" argument). The *Hellman* court noted that another jurisdiction, Maine, specifically required that its U.S. representatives be residents of the district that they represented, but that the requirement was not judicially challenged. The Supreme Court has never ruled on that question.

There are so few cases on this issue because representatives are, in fact, residents of the district that they represent. It is the historical custom of U.S. representatives to run from the district where they reside. When there is reapportionment of districts, incumbent congressmen who find themselves residents of the same district run against each other rather than trying to run in a district where they do not reside. Justice Story also noted that some states imposed, not only a district qualification, but a district residency qualification. Story, p. 100, sec. 624.

[24]*Statutes at Large*, vol. 5, p. 491, section 2 (1842). For the legislative history, see *Congressional Globe*, 2d Sess., App. 343, 493, 513 (1842).

though candidate A was the second highest vote-getter in a field of at least 20 candidates, 10 of whom will become U.S. representatives—candidate A still is not elected as a U.S. Representative, because he did not meet the *additional qualification* of obtaining the votes in the *right district*. That qualification is not found in article I, section 2, clause 2. It is found in the federal statute requiring that representatives be elected by district.

The most natural reading of the qualifications clause of article I, section 2, clause 2 is that it sets forth necessary, but not exclusive, qualifications for members of Congress. Other clauses in the Constitution impose additional qualifications,[25] while other portions of the Constitution place limits on the nature of any additional state or federal qualifications. A religious qualification,[26] for example, and a requirement that the voter or candidate be a property holder,[27] are examples of unconstitutional qualifications. They are unconstitutional, not because they violate the qualifications clause, but because they violate specific constitutional protections.

Another argument against the constitutionality of term limits relates to the qualifications of voters rather than the qualifications of candidates. Article I not only deals with the qualifications of the members of the House of Representatives, but also establishes the qualifications of the voters. However, it does not establish their qualifications directly. Rather, it incorporates and adopts the differing qualifications that the states have established: "the Electors in each State shall have the Qualifications requisite for Electors of the most numerous Branch of the State Legislature."[28] In other words,

---

[25]E.g., art. I, sec. 3, cl. 7 (impeached officials are disqualified from holding "any Office or honor, Trust, or Profit under the United States"); art. I, sec. 6, cl. 2 ("no Person holding any Office under the United States, shall be a Member of either House during his Continuance in Office"); art. II, sec. 1, cl. 2 (a presidential elector cannot be a U.S. senator or representative); Amendment XIV, sec. 3 (anyone who had taken an oath to support the Constitution and then "engaged in insurrection or rebellion against the same, or given aid or comfort to the enemies thereof" is disqualified to be a U.S. senator or representative unless Congress, by a two-thirds vote, removes "such disability").

[26]Art. VI, cl. 3 ("no religious Test shall ever be required as a Qualification."), and Amendment I ("Congress shall make no law respecting an establishment of religion, or prohibiting the free exercise thereof").

[27]E.g., *Hill v. Stone*, 421 U.S. 289 (1975) (interpreting the equal protection clause of the Fourteenth Amendment).

[28]Art. I, sec. 2, cl. 1.

whatever qualifications the state imposes on voters for state representative, the U.S. Constitution adopts as the voter qualification for U.S. representative. These qualifications can vary from state to state.

It may be easier to justify term limits in those cases where the state has imposed term limits on the most numerous branch of the state legislature. If a state, for example, has provided that no state legislator may serve more than six terms, the state is really saying that no voter in the state is allowed to vote (or is eligible to vote, or is qualified to vote) for a particular state legislator more than six terms. The voting clause of article I, section 2, clause 1 then kicks in to provide that the voters in our hypothetical state are similarly disqualified to vote for a member of the House of Representatives for more than six terms. The most obvious and simple way to enforce this voter qualification is to disqualify the candidate after six terms. If the voters are disqualified from voting for such a candidate, there is no reason to allow the candidate to run.

Does Supreme Court Case Law Forbid Term-Limit Legislation?

Opponents of laws that discourage or forbid long-term incumbency also base their constitutional objection on language in *Powell v. McCormack*.[29] Adam Clayton Powell, an outspoken black representative from Harlem, was accused of wrongfully diverting House funds for his own use, of asserting an unwarranted privilege and immunity from the processes of the New York courts, and of making false reports on expenditures of foreign currency to a House committee. After he was reelected to Congress, the House—amid charges that some members acted for racist reasons—voted to exclude him from the 90th Congress. It was admitted that Powell met the article I requirements of age, U.S. citizenship, and state residency. The Supreme Court ruled that it was unconstitutional for the House of Representatives to refuse to seat Representative Powell.

The Court found that the House had "excluded" Powell (pursuant to article I, section 5, clause 1, which requires a simple majority) rather than "expelled" him (pursuant to article I, section 5, clause 2, which requires a two-thirds majority). The Court decided that, even though the vote to expel a congressman might well be a "political question," with no judicial remedy,[30] the vote to exclude Powell

[29]395 U.S. 486 (1969).

[30]As Justice Douglas's separate opinion carefully explained, the Court would not have interfered if the House of Representatives had *expelled* Powell under a different

was not a political question, but was justiciable, and thus properly before the judiciary.

The difference between excluding a member (preventing him from sitting) and expelling a member (seating him and then throwing him out) was one of substance and not form for several reasons. First, many congressmen believed, in accordance with historical practice, that Congress could not expel a member, like Powell, whose wrongful activities occurred during a prior Congress. Some congressmen also admitted that, even though they voted to exclude Powell, they would not have voted to expel him.[31]

The Court ruled that the House of Representatives had acted unconstitutionally when it excluded Powell because the power of the House to exclude a member is narrower than its power to expel him. The power to expel, granted by the second clause of section 5 of article I, authorizes the House power to punish its members "for disorderly Behaviour." In contrast, the power to exclude (granted by the first clause of section 5 of article I) is a power to be used in connection with the power of Congress to judge the election returns of its members. Pursuant to that power, the House may only exclude a member who fails to meet the minimum requirements of age, U.S. citizenship, and state residency. Congress, said the Court—and this is the crucial point—cannot add to those qualifications in the guise of ad hoc discipline of its members. *Powell* did not concern itself with the power of *states* to impose term limits on members of Congress, or the power of states to enact ballot-access laws, or even with the power of *both* houses of Congress to enact a statute that imposed term limits.

In light of *Powell*, term-limits legislation would have to provide, explicitly or implicitly, for other methods of enforcement, such as

---

clause of the Constitution. Ibid., p. 546 and n. 8 (Opinion of Douglas, J., referring to art. I, sec. 5, cl. 2).

[31]While it was true that over two-thirds of the congressmen ended up voting to exclude Powell, that same number might not have voted to expel him. It is often the case in Congress that some members will not vote against something that will pass anyway, though they might take the political heat and vote against a proposal if their votes were truly needed. Thus, if something is going to pass anyway, it is often easier for its supporters to gather more than the necessary votes. The opponents of Powell, who thought that they only needed a simple majority to exclude him, could more easily exceed that modest target. But if everyone knew that they needed a two-thirds majority, that figure might not be attainable. It is one thing to cast a useless protest vote and quite another to defeat a proposal.

injunction, limitation of ballot access, and so forth. It could not rely on any supposed power of either house in judging election returns to enforce term limits by excluding members who meet the article I requirements. The Court did not consider, and did not hold, that both houses of Congress could not, by duly enacted statute, impose term limits. And it certainly did not even suggest that the *states*, and the people of the states, could not enact term-limits or ballot-access legislation. Such a question was not even before the *Powell* Court. While that interpretation of *Powell* is often criticized by term-limits opponents, it was confirmed by another Supreme Court opinion.[32]

Over the years, states have enacted a host of restrictions that govern and place qualifications on persons running for Congress. In each case, the states do not rely on either house of Congress to enforce those restrictions by exercising any supposed power to expel members by a simple majority. Thus, there is no violation of the *Powell* holding.

Some states prohibit candidates from holding certain other offices (the so-called resign-to-run rules) before running for Congress.[33] Some states require that candidates not be listed on the ballot unless they meet reasonable demonstrated-support or party-affiliation requirements.[34] Some states require that candidates win primaries.[35] Other states have barred write-in votes.[36] The Court has upheld such requirements if they are, in general, reasonable. There is no per se prohibition.[37]

[32]*Buckley v. Valeo*, 424 U.S. 1, 133 (1976) (per curiam), holding that art. I, sec. 5, confirms in Congress a power "judicial in character." Thus, Congress's power to legislate qualifications for office "must derive" from art. I, sec. 4.

[33]See, e.g., *Clements v. Fashing*, 457 U.S. 957 (1982) (resign-to-run); *Joyner v. Mofford*, 706 F.2d 1523, 1531 (9th Cir.), *cert. denied*, 464 U.S. 1002 (1983), where the court upheld a state constitutional provision that disqualified certain state officials from attempting to run for a federal office if the state officials remained in the state office. See also, *Signorelli v. Evans*, 637 F.2d 853, 859 (2d Cir. 1980), stating: "A state regulation, though it functions indirectly as a requirement for Congressional candidacy, may not necessarily be an unconstitutional additional qualification if it is designed to deal with a subject within traditional state authority."

[34]*Jenness v. Fortson*, 403 U.S. 431 (1971).

[35]*Munro v. Socialist Workers Party*, 479 U.S. 189, 197–98 (1986).

[36]*Burdick v. Takushi*, 112 S.Ct. 2059 (1992).

[37]See generally, Ronald D. Rotunda and John E. Nowak, *Treatise on Constitutional Law: Substance and Procedure*, 2nd ed. (St. Paul: West Publishing Co., 1992), vol. 3, secs. 18.31–18.33.

As the Supreme Court made clear in *Burdick v. Takushi*,[38] which upheld Hawaii's prohibition of write-in votes:

> When a state election law imposes only "reasonable, nondiscriminatory restrictions" upon first and fourteenth amendment rights of voters, the state's important regulatory interests are generally sufficient to justify the restrictions.[39]

Similarly, *Storer v. Brown*[40] upheld the constitutionality of various provisions of the California Elections Code that prohibited independent candidates from running in the general election if the candidates had either voted in an immediately preceding party primary or had registered their party affiliation with a qualified party within one year of the primary. Storer, one of the plaintiffs, was a registered Democrat whom the state thus disqualified for ballot status as an independent running for a seat in the U.S. Congress. The Court upheld the restrictions as reasonable and quickly dismissed an argument that a section of the California Election Code was "an additional qualification for office of Representative" and was thus "invalid under article I, section 2, clause 2." The Court said:

> The argument is wholly without merit. . . . The non-affiliation requirement no more establishes an additional requirement for the office of Representative than the requirement that the candidate win the primary to secure a place on the general ballot or otherwise demonstrate substantial community support.[41]

Those who claim that term limitation is unconstitutional (often, the claim is that term limitation is "clearly" or "obviously" unconstitutional) deal with these cases by explaining, for example, that a law disqualifying state judges from running for Congress (a resign-to-run law) is not really an added qualification for a U.S. representative. Rather, it is a resign-to-run rule. Similarly, a rule that prohibits one from being listed on the ballot as a congressional candidate unless there is a certain amount of demonstrated support is not really an added qualification; it is just a demonstrated-support rule.

[38]112 S.Ct. 2059 (1992).
[39]Ibid.
[40]415 U.S. 724 (1974).
[41]Ibid., p. 746 n. 16.

A rule prohibiting certain people from running for Congress because of the party-affiliation rules is not really an added qualification; it is just a party-affiliation requirement.[42] And so on. To some, the distinctions drawn may appear adroit, to others, specious.

If such reasoning is valid, it should be available to those who support the constitutionality of term limits. A rule limiting federal legislators to no more than, for example, 12 years (or 12 consecutive years) in office, is not really an added qualification; it is just a rule limiting the federal legislator to no more than 12 years (or 12 consecutive years) in office.

The lesson of *Powell* is that the power of the House of Representatives to use its quasi-judicial powers to exclude congressmen is limited; if the states have enacted reasonable qualifications for U.S. representatives in addition to those found in article I, section 2, clause 2, and those additional requirements do not violate other Constitutional clauses, then the states that have passed them should provide for their enforcement, and not rely on the House of Representatives using its narrow judicial power to exclude members.

Conclusion

Courts have consistently upheld a host of state restrictions on running for office. Those decisions recognize the states' wide discretion in regulating elections. The power to impose term limits or ballot-access requirements is really no more shocking than the power of the states to authorize a political party to require Presidential Electors to vote for the nominee of the party's national convention, in spite of the historical expectation by the Framers of the Constitution that the Presidential Electors would operate as free agents. Yet the Court has specifically approved of this state power over Presidential Electors.[43]

The Progressive movement, which flourished at the beginning of this century, was based on the assumption that the best cure for any perceived ills of democracy is more democracy. Thus, the Progressives gave us reforms such as the initiative, the referendum, and

[42]*Thorsted v. Gregoire*, 841 F.Supp. 1068 (1994), followed this traditional litany, by distinguishing all the prior restrictions on ballot access (such as resign-to-run rules, or demonstrated-support requirements) as not really added qualifications for office; only term limits, said the court—in a conclusory opinion bereft of any new arguments—are in the category of forbidden ballot-access rules.

[43]*Ray v. Blair*, 343 U.S. 214 (1952).

the recall of officeholders—all significantly changing political life, all enacted without constitutional amendment, and all resulting in a more responsive political branch. The move toward term limits for legislators is really a part of this legacy.

Index

Accountability
  of candidates and officeholders, 52, 55
  with term limits, 90–91
Adams, John, 60
Adams v. Supreme Court (1980), 102n18
Adverse selection, 12–13
Alex v. County of Los Angeles (1973), 102–3n18
American Party v. White (1974), 112n14
Ames, Fisher, 63–64
Anderson v. Celebrezze (1983), 122n57
Anti-Federalists
  concern for government without term limits, 104–5
  position on qualifications, 129
  representative government position, 74
  rotation in office concept of, 66–67, 84, 85
Aristotle, 34
Armor, John, 41
Articles of Confederation (1781), 16, 60–62, 102–3

Ballot access
  restrictions, 107, 142–43
  state laws related to, 112
Benjamin, Gerald, 92
Boorstin, Daniel, 75
Broadrick v. Oklahoma (1973), 122n58
Bronars, Stephen, 81
Buckingham v. State ex rel. Killoran (1944), 102n17
Buckley v. Valeo (1976), 121n53, 152
Burdick v. Takushi (1992), 112n15, 122nn56,57, 152n36, 153

Californians for Citizen Government v. Legislature (1992), 125n1
Campaign finance
  incumbents' solicitation, 141
  public funds as source of, 49
  rules created by legislators, 32
Campaign finance reform

  as alternative to term-limit solutions, 48–50
  expected outcome, 20
  incumbent protection provisions, 33
  public financing provision, 32
Canon, David, 81
Careers
  building, 72
  of congresspersons, 34, 35
  without term limits, 47
Cases of Contested Elections (1834), 106
Cicero, 34
Citizen action, 53, 55
Citizen legislature, 34–38, 43
Citizens. *See* Voters
Clements v. Fashing (1982), 118n42, 122n57, 152
Cobb v. State (1986), 102n17
Common Cause, 7, 38, 39, 69, 141
Common Cause, 39
Competition
  in congressional elections, 89–90, 94
  with term limits, 68, 80, 88
Congress
  as citizen legislature, 34–38, 43
  constitutional qualifications, 99–108
  current pattern of activity, 19
  effect of term limits on, 16, 19
  exemption from laws, 36
  power to override state election regulation, 116
  responsiveness of, 16
  with term limits, 20
Constitution, the (1787)
  absence of rotation principle, 62–65
  applied to term limits, 122–23
  article I, 110
  article I, section 2, clause 2, 113–14, 125, 146
  article I, section 3, clause 3, 113–14, 125
  article I, section 4, 116–18, 126
  article VI, clause 3, 146
  disqualifications clauses, 113–14

exclusivity of qualifications clauses,
   10, 99–108, 128–30
limits on state law making, 110–18
state control of voting qualifications,
   110, 115–16
term limits as violation, 110
Constitutional Convention (1787)
   mistrust of congressional
      incumbents, 116–17
   on qualifications of elected, 114–15
   term limit discussions and decisions,
      103–4
Courts
   Constitution as sole source of
      qualifications, 106–7
   states' inability to vary constitutional
      qualifications, 100–101
   striking down state-imposed
      qualifications, 101
   See also Supreme Court
Crane, Edward H., 34, 35, 74

Danielson v. Fitzsimmons (1950), 101n15
Democracy
   effect of term limits, 40, 94
   rotation in office as ingredient, 34–35
Demonstrated-support rule, 152–53
DeVeau v. Braisted (1960), 114n21
Dillon v. Fiorina (1972), 101n14
Dingell, Debbie, 29
Duggan v. Beerman (1992), 119n43

Education
   campaigns should provide, 51–52
   nonpartisan, political, 53–54
   political campaign role in, 51
Ekwall v. Stadelman (1934), 102n17
Election system
   barriers to participation, 54–55
   constitutional amendments to alter,
      110
   elections as term limits, 45
   incumbent reelection, 30
Entrepreneur, political, 19–20, 87–88
Eu v. San Francisco County Democratic
   Central Committee (1989), 139
Exclusivity
   in Constitution's article I, 10, 99–108,
      126–30
   Founders' intent, 99, 102–4
   Supreme Court interpretation, 143–44
   See also Powell v. McCormack (1969);
      Supreme Court
Executive, the, 16, 20

Exon v. Tiemann (1968), 101n14
Experience
   as argument for no term limits,
      75–82
   of new legislators, 79
   of new members of Congress, 79

Federalists, 74
Ferguson v. Skrupa (1963), 123n62
Fiorina, Morris, 87–88
Foley, Thomas S., 3–4, 109–10
Founders
   Article I intent for Congress, 20
   conception of representation, 73–74
   intent in exclusive qualifications for
      federal office, 99, 102–4
   intent in state regulation of elections,
      116–17
   position on term limits and rotation
      in office, 34–35, 85, 104–5
   rejection of term limits, 16–17, 62–67
   Wilson's criticism of, 21
Fourteenth Amendment, 106, 110
   applied to term limits, 121–22
   objections to term limits, 11
Fowler, Linda, 88
Framers. See Founders
Franking privilege, 30–31
Frenzel, Bill, 88–89
Fund, John, 63

Gerrymandering, 141
Gillam, Jerry, 42
Ginsberg, Benjamin, 69
Gobbler, Linda, 42
Goldwater, Barry, 23
Government
   American idea of republican, 18–19
   citizens' attitudes toward, 50–51
   private sector as source of, 13–14
   See also Representative government
Gregory v. Ashcroft (1991), 147

Hamilton, Alexander, 15, 65–67
   on definition of qualifications, 129
   on fixed and unalterable
      qualifications, 104, 115–16
   on state regulation of elections,
      116–17
   on wise legislator, 86
Heart of Atlanta Motel v. United States
   (1964), 111n7
Hellman v. Collier (1958), 101n14, 148
Hibbing, John, 77

Hill v. Stone (1975), 149
Hill v. Tucker (1993), 101n13, 119n44
Holmes, Oliver Wendell, Jr., 124
Hopfman v. Connolly (1984), 112n12

Incumbents
advantages of, 30–34, 69, 141
ballot access restrictions for long-
term, 142–43
Constitutional Convention mistrust
of, 116–17
effect of campaign finance reform on,
49–50
prolongation of office holding, 141
reelection power, 33–34
reelection rate, 30
reelection success, 69
responsiveness to constituency, 91
voting out, 45
Individualism, 93
INS v. Chadha (1983), 120n51

Jackley, John, 33–34
Jefferson, Thomas, 35, 61, 146–47
Jenness v. Fortson (1971), 112n14, 152n34
Joyner v. Mofford (1983), 99n5, 102n18,
134n22, 152n33

Kamber, Victor, 39, 76
Kent, James, 131
Kettering Foundation, 43, 51
Kunin, Madeleine, 37

League of Women Voters, 6, 7, 38, 39,
50, 52
Lee, Dwight R., 33
Lee, Richard Henry, 66–67
Legislation
campaign financing, 32
disqualifying, 113–14
Legislative power, state, 110–11
Legislators
activity related to tenure and
seniority, 77–78
dependence on PAC funding, 32
See also Incumbents; Representatives
Legislature v. Eu (1991), 112n13, 117n32,
125n1
Leonard v. Smith (1993), 119n45
Lincoln, Abraham, 35, 74
Lochner v. New York (1905), 123n60
Logrolling, legislative, 13
Lott, John, 81
Lowe v. Fowler (1977), 102n17
Lyons, Henry, 42

McCreery, William, 100
McGovern, George, 36–37
Madison, James
addition of new House members, 109
consideration of qualifications, 104
fixed qualifications, 115–16
public institutions and public
opinion, 22, 85–86
qualifications of electors and elected,
115, 128–29
relation of representative to
constituents, 35
states' regulation of federal elections,
116
Malbin, Michael, 92
Mann, Thomas, 38, 43, 68, 70–71
Media role, 52–53
Miyazawa v. City of Cincinnati (1993),
121n54
Morehead v. New York ex rel. Tipaldo
(1936), 123n60
Morris, Gouverneur, 128
Munro v. Socialist Workers Party (1986),
112n14, 152n35

National Voter Registration Act, 55
The New York Times, 76

In re O'Connor (1940), 101n15, 102n16
Oklahoma State Election Board v. Coats
(1980), 102–3n18
Ornstein, Norman, 80

Party-affiliation rule, 152–54
Payne, James, 80
Pearce, Trudy, 31
Plante v. Smith, 119n46
Plugge v. McCuen (1992), 101n13
Political action committees (PACs)
funding to incumbents, 32
proposal to limit contributions of, 49
Political campaigns
as forum for discussion, 51
needed reform, 50–52
Polsby, Nelson W., 76–77
Post-It® Brand Tape flags, 50–51
Powell v. McCormack (1969), 94, 99–100,
118–21
confirmation in *Buckley v. Valeo*
(1976), 152
defines negative implication, 134
misinterpretation, 11
resolution of qualifications clause
ambiguity, 127–32, 135, 140,
150–52

Presidency, the
  constitutional weakness of, 20
  reflection of person holding office,
    20–21
  turnover in officeholders, 141
  See also Executive, the
Price, Charles, 79
Price, David, 75–76
Private sector, 13–14
Professionalism
  of politics, 73
  requirement for, 87–88
  of state legislatures, 69, 79–80
  term limits as antidote to, 59, 72–75,
    84–85
  trend in politics, 8
Professional representation, 74–75
Public Citizen, Inc. v. Miller (1993), 99n5

Qualifications
  article I, section 2, clause 2, 143–46
  article VI, clause 3, 146, 147–48
  Congressional power to judge, 101
  Constitutional disqualifications, 11,
    145
  language in Constitution, 125
  natural reading of article I, section 2,
    clause 2, 149
  objection to state-level laws (Story),
    114
  requirement of states to impose
    district, 148–49
  state restrictions on, 152
  states cannot add to constitutional,
    100
  unconstitutional, 149
  voter qualifications, 149–50
  See also Ballot access; Constitution,
    the (1787);
  Resign-to-run statutes
Quasi-term limits, 126, 134–40

Randolph, Edmund, 114–15
Ray v. Blair (1952), 154n43
Reed, W. Robert, 80
Reelection
  incumbent advantages, 30, 33–34,
    69–70
  legislators' seeking, 69–70
  See also Turnover
Registration barriers, 54
Remini, Robert V., 17n2
Reno v. Flores (1993), 123n62

Representative government
  effect of professionalization of, 73–75
  experience required, 75–82
Representatives
  amateurs as legislators, 81, 92
  district qualification requirement,
    148–49
  eligibility for leadership in
    legislature, 80
  professionalization of, 72–75
Resign-to-run statutes, 102, 152–53
Richardson v. Hare (1968), 102n17
Riley v. Cordell (1948), 102n17
Rodriguez v. Popular Democratic Party
    (1982), 122n56
Roe v. Wade, 123n61
Rotation, mandatory. See Term limits
Rotation in office
  advantages, 61–62
  effect of mandatory, 84–88
  historical idea of, 7, 34–35, 59–67
  opposition, 65–66
  principle in American history, 59–61
  term limits to underscore principle
    of, 58–59
  voluntary, 64–65
  See also Term limits
Roth v. Cuevas (1993), 121n55
Roudebush v. Hartke (1972), 118n35
Ruling and being ruled, 81

Schansberg, D. Eric, 80
Seniority system
  effect of eliminating, 93
  function of, 77–78
  power in Congress with, 38
  relation of spending to, 80
Seventeenth Amendment, 58; 117
Shefter, Martin, 69
Shub v. Simpson (1950), 102n16
Signorelli v. Evans (1980), 99n5, 102n18,
    133nn20,21
Smiley v. Holm (1932), 118n35
Smith v. Ehrlich (1976), 122n59
Special interests, 48–50
Squire, Peverill, 79
Stack v. Adams (1970), 102n17, 131n12
State ex rel. Chandler v. Howell (191918),
    102n17
State ex rel. Chavez v. Evans (1968),
    101n14
State ex rel. Eaton v. Schmahl (1918),
    101n15

State ex rel. Handley v. Superior Court (1958), 102n17
State ex rel. Johnson v. Crane (1948), 106n42
State ex rel. Pickrell v. Senner (1962), 102n16
State ex rel. Santini v. Swackhamer (1974), 101n13, 102n17
State ex rel. Watson v. Cobb (1863), 102–3n18
State ex rel. Wettengel v. Zimmerman (1946), 102n17, 136nn25,26
States
    district qualifications, 148–49
    legislative power of, 110–18
    term-limit legislation, 3, 37n35, 57, 111–12
    See also Qualifications; Term limit laws
Stockton v. MacFarland (1940), 102n17
Storer v. Brown (1974), 112n14, 117n34, 119n46, 130, 132-33, 137-38, 142-43n5, 153
Story, Joseph, 12
    on article I, section 3, 64
    exclusivity of qualifications clause, 11, 146
    influence of interpretation of article I, 118, 131
    objection to state qualification laws, 114
Strong v. Breaux (1992), 101n14
Stumpf v. Lau (1992), 101n13, 119n44
Supreme Court
    changing interpretations of Constitution, 123
    interpretation using exclusivity criterion, 99–100, 143–44
    Powell v. Mc Cormack, 94, 99–100, 118–21, 134, 152
    upholding of write-in option, 112

Tashjian v. Republican Party of Connecticut (1986), 139
Tenth Amendment, 110–11
Tenure
    effect of, 75–82
    electoral safety with, 80
    rise of Congressional members, 41
Term limit laws
    city-level, 27, 29, 57, 125
    move to declare unconstitutional, 3–4
    restrict long-term incumbents, 142–43
    state-level, 27–29, 57, 125

Thorsted v. Gregoire, 101, 107
    See also Thorsted v. Gregoire (1994); *U. S. Term Limits v. Hill*
Term limits
    arguments against, 29, 38–41, 45–48, 75–82, 89–95, 149–50
    arguments for, 12, 28–34, 57–58, 68–72, 75–82, 84–86, 88, 126
    campaigns against initiatives, 3, 38–41
    to change motives, 22–23
    Constitution applied to, 122–23
    effectiveness, 41–43, 92
    effect of differences in form of, 87
    effect on Congress, 16, 19
    Fourteenth Amendment applied to, 121–22
    goals of, 37–38, 40
    impact on incumbent advantage, 33–34
    on office of president, 29
    pre-federal Constitutions, 59–62, 102–3
    rejection by Constitutional Convention, 16–17, 62–67
    to underscore rotation in office principle, 58–59
    See also Constitution, the (1787); Qualifications; Quasi-term limits; Rotation in office
Term limits, state-level
    initiatives, 3, 37n35, 41–42
    laws enacted, 111–12
    in place, 57
Thorsted v. Gregoire (1994), 3–4, 101n13, 102n18, 107n46, 110n3, 119n46, 125, 143n6, 154n42
Tocqueville, Alexis de, 21
Tulis, Jeffrey, 20
Turnover
    changes in incidence, 70–72
    levels in Congress (1974–92), 89
    for the presidency, 141
    in Senate compare to House, 141
Twenty-Second Amendment, 141

U. S. Term Limits, 4, 6, 9
U. S. Term Limits v. Hill, 119n44
United Pub. Workers v. Mitchell (1947), 122n58
United States Civil Service Commission v. National Association of Letter Carriers (1973), 122n58

United States v. Classic (1941), 117n33
United States v. Richmond (1982), 101n15

Virginia Bill of Rights, 60
Virginia Plan, 103
Voters
   as judge of interests served, 46, 94
   need to encourage, 54–55
   qualifications at state level, 115–16
   role in political debate, 53
Voting qualifications, 149–50

Warren, Earl, 94, 119
Washington, George, 64

Wertheimer, Fred, 69
White, Byron, 137–38
Wickard v. Filburn (1942), 111n7
Will, George, 4–5, 36, 85–87, 91, 92–93
Williamson, Hugh, 104
Williams v. Rhodes (1968), 137
Williams v. Tucker (1974), 148
Wilson, James, 63
Write-in vote
   with restricted access to long-term
      incumbents, 142–43
   Supreme Court decisions, 112

Zinerman v. Burch (1990), 123n62

Contributors

Becky Cain is president of the League of Women Voters of the United States.

Edward H. Crane is president of the Cato Institute.

Lloyd N. Cutler is senior counsel to the Washington, D.C. law firm of Wilmer, Cutler & Pickering.

Paul Jacob is executive director of U.S. Term Limits.

John G. Kester is a partner in the Washington, D.C. law firm of Williams & Connolly.

Daniel H. Lowenstein is a professor of law at the University of California, Los Angeles.

Thomas E. Mann is director of the Governmental Studies Program at the Brookings Institution.

Mark P. Petracca is an associate professor of political science at the University of California, Irvine.

Roger Pilon is director of the Cato Institute's Center for Constitutional Studies.

Ronald D. Rotunda is the Albert E. Jenner, Jr., professor of law at the University of Illinois College of Law.

George F. Will is a syndicated columnist with the *Washington Post* and a contributing editor of *Newsweek* magazine.

Cato Institute

Founded in 1977, the Cato Institute is a public policy research foundation dedicated to broadening the parameters of policy debate to allow consideration of more options that are consistent with the traditional American principles of limited government, individual liberty, and peace. To that end, the Institute strives to achieve greater involvement of the intelligent, concerned lay public in questions of policy and the proper role of government.

The Institute is named for *Cato's Letters*, libertarian pamphlets that were widely read in the American Colonies in the early 18th century and played a major role in laying the philosophical foundation for the American Revolution.

Despite the achievement of the nation's Founders, today virtually no aspect of life is free from government encroachment. A pervasive intolerance for individual rights is shown by government's arbitrary intrusions into private economic transactions and its disregard for civil liberties.

To counter that trend, the Cato Institute undertakes an extensive publications program that addresses the complete spectrum of policy issues. Books, monographs, and shorter studies are commissioned to examine the federal budget, Social Security, regulation, military spending, international trade, and myriad other issues. Major policy conferences are held throughout the year, from which papers are published thrice yearly in the *Cato Journal*. The Institute also publishes the quarterly magazine *Regulation*.

In order to maintain its independence, the Cato Institute accepts no government funding. Contributions are received from foundations, corporations, and individuals, and other revenue is generated from the sale of publications. The Institute is a nonprofit, tax-exempt, educational foundation under Section 501(c)3 of the Internal Revenue Code.

CATO INSTITUTE
1000 Massachusetts Ave., N.W.
Washington, D.C. 20001